Götz Maier-Dörner

Englisch

Gymnasium 8. Schuljahr

TRAINING

Klett Lernen und Wissen

Götz Maier-Dörner ist Gymnasiallehrer in Baden-Württemberg für die Fächer Englisch, Geschichte und Gemeinschaftskunde.

Zu diesem Trainingsbuch gehört eine Audio-CD. Mit ihrer Hilfe lernst du, Englisch besser zu verstehen. Die Texte sind im Buch mit dem Symbol gekennzeichnet. Wenn du die Aufgaben bearbeitest, benutze die Pausentaste, um Zeit zum Schreiben zu haben. Viel Erfolg!

Aufnahmestudio: Noah-Studios, Hannover
Sprecher: Jennifer Turk, Hamburg; Dave Mancini, Hannover; John Symon, Barsinghausen

Bibliographische Information Der Deutschen Bibliothek
Die Deutsche Bibliothek verzeichnet diese Publikation in der Deutschen Nationalbibliographie; detaillierte bibliographische Daten sind im Internet über http://dnb.ddb.de abrufbar.

Auflage 4. 3. 2. 1. | 2011 2010 2009 2008
Die letzten Zahlen bezeichnen jeweils die Auflage und das Jahr des Druckes.
Dieses Werk folgt der reformierten Rechtschreibung und Zeichensetzung. Ausnahmen bilden Texte, bei denen künstlerische, philologische oder lizenzrechtliche oder andere Gründe einer Änderung entgegenstehen.

Internetadresse: www.klett.de
Zeichnungen: Naomi Fearn, Berlin: S. 9, 99, 100, 104, 119; Marlene Pohle, Stuttgart: S. 100, 104; Katja Wesner, Fellbach: S. 29, 54, 60, 70, 71, 92, 120, 133
Umschlaggestaltung: VIER FÜR TEXAS Ideenwerk, Frankfurt/Main
Redaktion: Elisabeth Dorner, Berlin
Satz: Klaus Bauer, Bondorf
Reproduktion: Meyle + Müller, Medien-Management, Pforzheim
Druck: Mediahaus Biering GmbH, München
Printed in Germany.
ISBN: 978-3-12-927072-1

Vorwort

Grammar

5 Modal auxiliaries and their replacements 64

6 Reported speech 78

Vocabulary

7 American and British English 100

8 Building words 108

Understanding English

9 Reading comprehension 120

10 Listening comprehension 130

Lösungen 141

Inhalt der Audio-CD 189

Register 190

Liebe Eltern,

mit *Training Englisch Gymnasium 8. Schuljahr* haben Sie eine Lernhilfe für Ihr Kind erworben, die nach neuesten methodisch-didaktischen Prinzipien konzipiert wurde und sich an den neuen Lehr- und Bildungsplänen orientiert.

Alle Übungen sind selbst zu korrigieren und gut verständlich aufbereitet. Das Buch eignet sich zum Wiederholen, Vertiefen oder zum gezielten Arbeiten an erkannten Schwächen.

Jedes Kapitel für sich behandelt nicht nur ein sprachliches Phänomen, sondern ist auch **inhaltlich einem Thema gewidmet** (z. B. „Ein Besuch in Chicago"). Eintönige Übungen mit inhaltlich nicht zusammenhängenden Sätzen werden dadurch vermieden.

Neben dem klassischen Schwerpunkt **Grammatik** kann Ihr Kind auch **Vokabular** sowie das **Hör- und Leseverstehen** üben und lernt dabei **Methoden für den Umgang mit Vokabeln und Lese- sowie Hörverstehenstexten**. Als zusätzliches Training des Hörverstehens und der Aussprache sind alle Dialoge, die im Buch vorkommen, aufgenommen. Gerade die sogenannte Methodenkompetenz hat in den letzten Jahren in den Schulen an Bedeutung gewonnen, da sie über das einzelne Problem hinaus als Handwerkszeug zum Lösen von Problemen generell dient.

Innerhalb der Grammatik haben wir gezielt die Bereiche ausgewählt, die den Schülerinnen und Schülern in der Regel besondere Schwierigkeiten bereiten. Sollten Sie ein Thema in diesem Band vermissen, so finden Sie es vermutlich in dem vorhergehenden oder dem nachfolgenden Band dieser Reihe.

Wir wünschen Ihren Kindern und Ihnen selbst viel Erfolg und Freude mit der englischen Sprache.

Liebe Schülerin, lieber Schüler,

dieses Buch mit Audio-CD hilft dir, in Englisch fit zu werden. Du kannst es von Anfang bis Ende durcharbeiten oder dir einzelne Kapitel vornehmen, weil ihr sie vielleicht gerade im Unterricht hattet und darüber eine Klassenarbeit schreibt, oder einfach nur, weil sie dich interessieren.

Das Buch ist in **drei Hauptkapitel** unterteilt:

1. Grammar
Hier werden ausgewählte Grammatikthemen erklärt und geübt.

2. Vocabulary
Hier lernst du bestimmte Wortfelder kennen, aber auch, wie man bestimmte Wörter, die du schon kennst, richtig anwendet. Außerdem findest du hier viele Tipps, die dir das Vokabellernen erleichtern werden.

3. Understanding English
Hier kannst du üben, geschriebene und gesprochene Texte zu verstehen. Für dieses Kapitel benötigst du die CD. Auf der CD findest du auch alle Dialoge, die im Buch vorkommen. Hörverstehensübungen sind im Buch mit dem Symbol gekennzeichnet.

Die einzelnen Kapitel sind immer gleich aufgebaut:

Check-up
Hier kannst du überprüfen, wie viel du über ein Thema noch weißt.

Wissen
Hier werden die wichtigsten Regeln noch einmal mit Beispielen erklärt.

Üben
Hier kannst du üben, was du gerade gelernt hast.

Test
Hier kannst du überprüfen, ob du das Thema verstanden hast.

Am Ende der Hauptkapitel findest du eine Seite zur Selbsteinschätzung, eine **Checkliste**. Mit ihrer Hilfe kannst du selbst noch einmal darüber nachdenken, wie viel du gelernt hast, und entscheiden, ob du zum nächsten Kapitel weitergehen oder lieber noch einmal wiederholen möchtest.

Und nun: Viel Erfolg und hoffentlich auch viel Spaß beim Lernen.

Grammar

WHY DO WE NEED GRAMMAR?
WELL, YOU SEE, TO MAKE A SENTENCE, YOU NEED TO PUT WORDS TOGETHER IN THE RIGHT ORDER.
IF YOU JUST STICK ANY WORDS TOGETHER, THEY DON'T MEAN ANYTHING.
NOT EVEN IF I MAKE THEM LOOK LIKE A DOGGY?
NO, I'M AFRAID NOT.

1 The past perfect simple and progressive

1.1 The past perfect simple

1 Check-up

Complete the sentences with the verb in the past perfect simple.

More than 20,000 years ago the first immigrants came to America across the Bering Strait. This was long after the first animals *had travelled* (travel) the same way looking for food. Yet, after Christopher Columbus ______________________ (discover) America in 1492, life for the 1.5 million Native Americans, whom Columbus ______________________ (call) Indians, changed a lot. After news of the "New World" ______________________ (reach) Europe, thousands of people followed Columbus across the Atlantic to start a new life. Before the settlers from Europe came, most Native American tribes ______________________ (live) nomadic lives. Now people with two different ways of life had to share the land, and that of course led to many conflicts. After Indians and Europeans ______________________ (fight) many wars and thousands of people ______________________ (die), the Indians finally had to accept that they ______________________ (lose). Of the 1.5 million Native Americans who ______________________ (live) in America when Columbus arrived in 1492, only 350,000 remained in 1920. The nomads who 200 years earlier ______________________ (hunt) buffaloes now lived on reservations.

Das *past perfect simple*

Im Englischen werden Geschichten, die in der Vergangenheit spielen, meist im *simple past* erzählt. Aber auch in der Vergangenheit kommt es vor, dass eine Handlung vor einer anderen stattgefunden hat. Um dies zu beschreiben, verwendet man das *past perfect* (Plusquamperfekt oder auch Vorvergangenheit). Im Deutschen sagt man „hatte" oder „war" (ich hatte entdeckt, ich war gereist).

Bildung des *past perfect*

had + past participle
had travelled
had discovered

Das *past perfect* kommt meist im Zusammenhang mit dem *past tense* vor. Sehr oft stehen auch die **Signalwörter *before*** und ***after*** im gleichen Satz. Wichtig bei der Verwendung des *past perfect* ist genau zu überlegen, was zuerst passierte und was später.

früher (past perfect)	**später (past tense)**
After Christopher Columbus **had discovered** America in 1492,	life for the 1.5 million Native Americans **changed** a lot.
Most Native American tribes **had lived** nomadic lives	**before** the settlers from Europe came.

Die Reihenfolge von Haupt- und Nebensatz ist frei wählbar. Man kann also auch sagen:

später	**früher**
Life for the 1.5 million Native Americans **changed** a lot	**after** Christopher Columbus **had discovered** America in 1492.
Before the settlers from Europe came,	most Native American tribes **had lived** nomadic lives.

Beachte dabei, dass immer dann ein Komma zwischen Haupt- und Nebensatz steht, wenn der Nebensatz (eingeleitet durch *after* oder *before*) zuerst steht.

2

Read part 1 of this Native American story. Then fill in the gaps, using *before* or *after*.

The origin of fire

A long, long time ago, animals and trees talked with each other, but there was no fire.
Fox was the most clever animal, and he tried to think of a way to create fire for the world. So he decided to visit the geese, and told them he wanted to learn how to imitate their cry. They promised to teach him, if he flew with them. So they gave wings to Fox, but told him never to open his eyes while flying.
On one of their flights, darkness came suddenly, and the geese saw the village of the fireflies* below. The flickering fireflies made Fox open his eyes, and right away he fell to the ground and into the walled area of the firefly village, where a fire constantly burned in the centre.

* **firefly** – Glühwürmchen

1. Fox had tried to think of a way to create fire ______________ he decided to visit the geese.
2. ______________ they had told him that they would teach him their cry, they gave him wings so he could fly with them.
3. But ______________ they attached the wings, they had also told him never to open his eyes while flying.
4. The geese saw the village of the fireflies ______________ darkness had come.
5. Fox had opened his eyes ______________ he fell into the firefly village.

3

Read part 2 of "The origin of fire". Then fill in the gaps using the correct form of the verbs (simple past or past perfect simple).

The origin of fire (part 2)

Two friendly fireflies came to help fallen Fox, and he gave each one a necklace[1] of juniper berries[2], because he hoped to persuade them to tell him how he could find a way over the wall to the outside. They led him to a cedar tree[3], which they explained would bend down upon command and catapult[4] him over the wall if he wanted. Fox was glad to know this. He stayed in the village for the next few days, and became friends with the fireflies.
Then one evening Fox suggested to the fireflies, "Let's have a festival where we can dance, and I will produce the music." They all agreed that that would be fun and helped to gather wood to build up a greater fire. Secretly, Fox tied a piece of cedar bark[5] to his tail. Then he made a drum and beat a rhythm on it with a stick for the dancing fireflies. Slowly, he moved closer and closer to the fire. After a while, Fox pretended to tire from beating the drum and gave it to some fireflies who wanted to help make the music. Fox quickly held his tail into the fire, lighting the bark, and said: "It is too warm here for me, I must find a cooler place."
Then he started running to the cedar tree, shouting: "Bend down to me, my cedar tree, bend down!"

1 **necklace** – Kette; 2 **juniper berries** – Wacholderbeeren; 3 **cedar tree** – Zeder;
4 **catapult** – schleudern; 5 **bark** – Rinde

1. After two friendly fireflies ____________________ **(come)** to help fallen Fox, he ________________ **(give)** each one of them a necklace of juniper berries.

2. After they ____________________ **(lead)** him to the cedar tree, they ____________________________ **(explain)** that it would catapult him over the wall if he wanted.

3. Fox _________________________ **(become)** friends with the fireflies after he _________________________ **(stay)** in the village for a few days.

4. Before the fireflies __________________ **(help)** to gather wood to build a greater fire, they __________________ **(agree)** that a festival would be fun.

5. Fox __________________ **(tie)** a piece of bark to his tail before he __________________ **(build)** a drum and __________________ **(beat)** a rhythm on it for the dancing flies.

6. After he __________________ **(start)** to beat the drum, he __________________ **(move)** slowly closer and closer to the fire.

7. He __________________ **(pretend)** to tire from beating the drum before he __________________ **(give)** the drum to some fireflies.

8. Before he __________________ **(say)**: "It's too warm here for me, I must find a cooler place," he __________________ **(hold)** his tail into the fire, lighting the bark.

9. After he __________________ **(start)** running to the cedar tree, he __________________ **(shout)**: "Bend down to me, my cedar tree, bend down!"

4

Read part 3 of "The origin of fire". Then connect the sentences, using *after* or *before* and the correct tenses.

The origin of fire (part 3)

The cedar tree bent down for Fox to catch hold of it, then it carried him up far over the wall. He landed on the other side and started running. On and on he ran, with the fireflies following him.
Fox ran past trees and bushes and they started to burn from the sparks[1] dropping from the burning bark tied to his tail.
Finally Fox became tired and gave the burning bark to Hawk, who carried it to brown Crane[2]. He flew far to the south, dropping fire sparks everywhere so that fires started burning all over the earth.
The fireflies chased Fox all the way to his den[3] and said, "Forever after, Wily[4] Fox, your punishment for stealing our fire will be that you can never make use of it for yourself."
For the Apache nation, this too was the origin of fire. First they learned to control it, and soon afterwards they used it for cooking their food, and to keep themselves warm in cold weather.

1 **spark** – Funke; 2 **crane** – Kranich; 3 **den** – Bau; 4 **wily** – schlau

Example:
The cedar tree bent down. It carried Fox up far over the wall.
After the cedar tree had bent down, it carried Fox high over the wall.

or

The cedar tree carried Fox high over the wall after it had bent down.

or

Before it carried Fox high over the wall, the cedar tree had bent down.

or

The cedar tree had bent down before it carried Fox high over the wall.

1. Fox landed on the other side. He started running.

____

____

____

____

2. Fox ran past trees and bushes. They started to burn from the sparks dropping from the bark on his tail.

3. Fox became tired. He gave the bark to Hawk who carried it to brown Crane.

4. He flew far to the south, dropping sparks everywhere. Fires started burning all over the earth.

5. The fireflies chased Fox all the way to his den. They said: "You will never be able to make use of the fire."

6. The Apache nation learned to control fire. They used it for cooking and to keep themselves warm in cold weather.

1.2 The past perfect progressive

5 Check-up

Fill in the gaps in the past perfect progressive, using the verbs in brackets.

Mick Mitchell travelled the Oregon California trail in 1849. This is part of his diary:

Before I left New York I ______________________________ **(work)** at a butcher's since 1846, when I had arrived in the New World. It was terrible. When I got up in the mornings at 4 o'clock, I had only slept for 5 hours, because we ______________________________ **(work)** from 6 o'clock a.m. until 8 o'clock p.m. every day, and I had a long way to go to get to work. I ______________________________ **(do)** this for two years when I decided that I had to get away. In that time I received a letter from a friend who ______________________________ **(live)** in California for two years. He wrote that he had just found gold. So I decided to take my chances, too. I ______________________________ **(save)** money for some time so that I had enough to start the trip. But now I'm lost in the middle of the wilderness, and I'm starting to think that the butcher's in New York wasn't so bad after all …

Das *past perfect progressive*

had been	**+**	**-ing-Form**
had been		working
had been		sleeping

Verwendung

Die Verwendung des *past perfect progressive* versteht man am besten, wenn man es mit der anderer Vergangenheitsformen vergleicht.
Das *past perfect progressive* beschreibt nämlich Handlungen, die in der Vorvergangenheit lange andauerten – ob sie an einem bestimmten Punkt endeten oder nicht, spielt jedoch keine Rolle. Die Handlungen des *present perfect progressive* (*have been doing*) dagegen dauern lange an und reichen in die Gegenwart hinein.
Ähnlich wie beim *present perfect progressive* begegnet man beim *past perfect progressive* sehr oft ***for*** und ***since*** als **Signalwörtern**.

I **had been working** at a butcher's **since** 1846 before I left New York.
Ich hatte seit 1846 in der Metzgerei gearbeitet, bevor ich New York verließ.

Ähnlich wie beim *past progressive* (*were doing*) tritt oft während der im *past perfect progressive* beschriebenen Handlung eine andere Handlung ein, die im *simple past* steht.

I **had been working** there **for** two years **when I decided** that I had to get away.
Ich hatte dort seit zwei Jahren gearbeitet, als ich mich dazu entschied wegzugehen.

Das *past perfect progressive* betont dabei, dass eine Handlung **vor** einer anderen Handlung (im *simple past*) begonnen hat. (Vorzeitigkeit: Ich hatte seit zwei Jahren dort gearbeitet, als …).

Das *past progressive* betont dagegen die Gleichzeitigkeit der Handlungen (*while* = während).

While I **was working** at the butcher's, my best friend was run over by a car.

Beachte:
Intransitive Verben wie *know*, *want*, *love*, *realise*, *understand*, *believe*, *remember*, *seem*, *hate*, die keine Handlung beschreiben, werden normalerweise nicht in der Verlaufsform (*progressive form*) verwendet.

Übersicht: Verlaufsformen der Vergangenheit

Present perfect progressive:
I've been living in New York for 6 years.

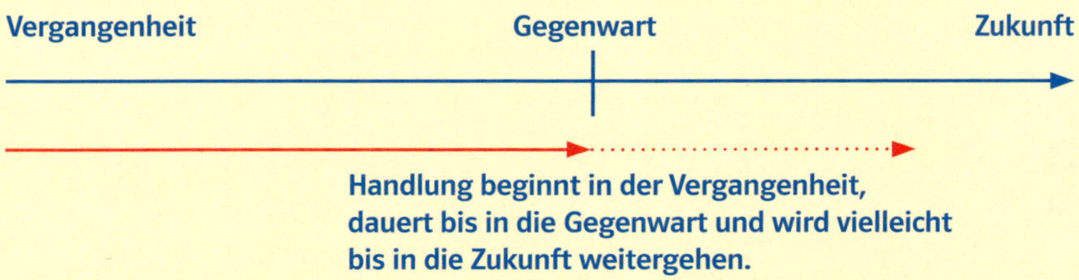

Past progressive:
While I **was working** at the butcher's, **my best friend was run over** by a car.

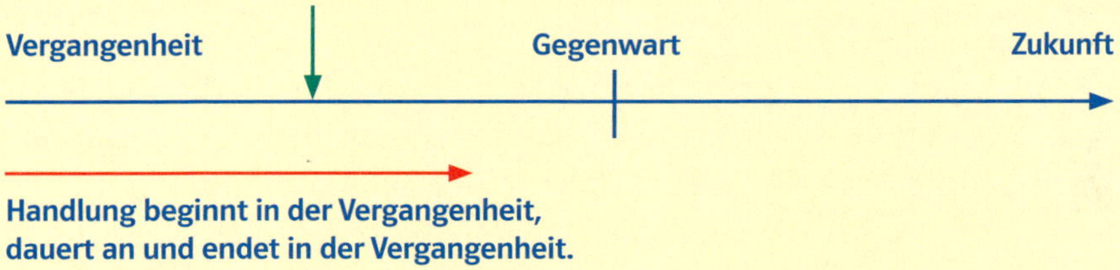

Oft tritt, während eine Handlung stattfindet, eine weitere Handlung ein, die dann im ***simple past*** steht.

Past perfect progressive:
I **had been working** ... since 1846 **before I left New York**.

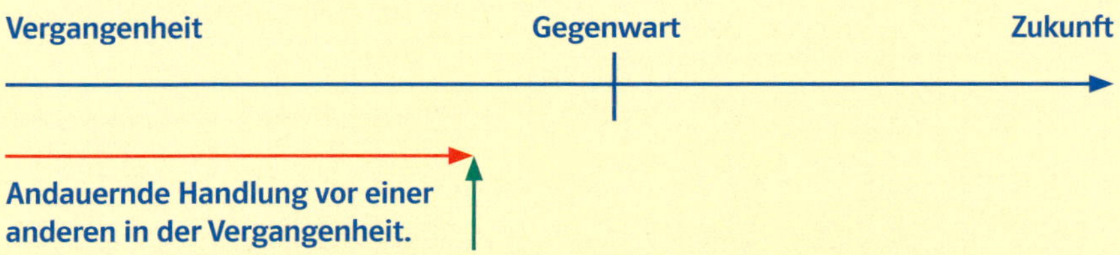

Übungen zum *present perfect progressive* und *past progressive* findest du im Band für das 7. Schuljahr, Kapitel 3 und 4.

6 1

Complete the sentences in the past perfect progressive, using the verbs from the box. You can listen to the CD to check your answers.

graze[1]	fight	scout[2]	dream	follow	look

Talk on the trail

1. *Phil:* You look very tired, Sue.

   Sue: Yes, I had only slept two hours when the trumpet was blown.

   Phil: Why was that?

   Sue: I ________________________ of attacking Indians and couldn't go back to sleep afterwards.

2. *Alex:* Did you check on the cattle last night?

   Joe: Yeah, they ________________________ peacefully since we left them but they were a little nervous later on. There might have been a bear out there.

3. *Marie:* We're late starting this morning, mom.

   Mrs. Morris: I told you, it's because the men ________________________ more carefully. They thought that there might have been some Indians out there.

4. *Phil:* I've just come back from hunting. What happened to Mitchell?

   Alex: He had just found the fresh water he ________________________ for all morning when a puma appeared and attacked him. Mitchell and the puma ________________________ for a few minutes already when Joe came just in time to save Mitchell's life. How about you, did you shoot anything?

   Phil: No, I ________________________ a herd of buffaloes for three hours when they saw me and ran away.

1 to graze – grasen; **2 to scout** – auskundschaften

7

Complete the sentences with the verbs in the correct tense: past perfect simple or progressive?

Mick Mitchell's diary after the trip

We have finally made it. It was terrible. After we ______________________ (leave) New York, everything seemed to be fine. But then many crazy things happened. One morning I woke up and saw that it ______________________ ______________________ (rain) all night. However, it ________________ just ________________ (stop), so I jumped out of the wagon and realized that it was almost impossible to walk because of all the mud. We also quickly realized that it would be difficult to move the wagons. We were only able to move again after we ______________________________ (push) and ______________________________ (pull) for three hours. We also had to shoot a cow that ______________________________ (break) its leg. It ______________________________ (try) to get out of a big puddle when it somehow tripped, fell and hurt itself. A few days later I was attacked by a puma because I ______________________________ (not be) careful enough. I ______________________________ (look) for water when it suddenly appeared out of the woods. I ________________ ________________ (fight) the puma with my bare hands for a few minutes when Joe came and shot it. I am really happy to be in my new home now: California!

8

Past perfect progressive or past progressive?

Complete the sentences using the phrases below.

He had been digging for gold for only a few weeks

while he was talking,

after he'd been travelling in the wilderness for two years,

While he was sitting next to the river, thinking how life might go on,

The rich man was looking for strong men

had been looking for gold for about three months without success

what Mick had been doing for the past few years.

How Mick Mitchell left California

After Mick ______________________________

______________________________,

he decided to give up. He had to realise that all the good claims* had been taken by other diggers already. ______________________________

____

____

a rich-looking man started talking to him. He wanted to know ______________________________

____

______________________________.

So Mick told him his story, and ______________________________

____

the man became more and more interested. ______________________

____

who had already travelled the Oregon trail. ____________________

____

____

and now wanted to take his gold back to New York. However, he needed men to protect him from robbers. Mick decided to accept the job because the man promised him a lot of money. When Mick arrived in New York ____________

____

____

he had to find work with a butcher once again. The rich man had never paid him, and was never heard of again.

*__claim__ – Schürfstelle

1

Correct the mistakes. There is one mistake in each sentence.

The story of Pocahontas

Pocahontas was the daughter of an Indian chieftain who tried to keep peace between Europeans and Indians.

1. Pocahontas was still a child when the first settlers were arriving in Virginia.

   ____

2. Pocahontas had always was a very curious child and therefore she wanted to get to know these strange white people.

   ____

3. After Pocahontas have saved the life of an English prisoner, the settlers started to like her.

   ____

4. Before she marries an English colonist, she had become a Christian.

   ____

5. The relationship between the English and Pocahontas' tribe was becoming more peaceful after she had married a colonist.

   ____

points: *one point for each mistake*

2

Complete the sentences with the verbs in the correct tense: simple past, past perfect simple or past perfect progressive?

After Pocahontas ________________________ **(learn)** the English language she ________________________ **(make)** friends among the settlers. However, when war ________________________ **(break)** out between the settlers and Pocahontas' tribe, she was taken prisoner. When her father ______________________ (refuse) to pay ransom[1] for her, the English ______________________ (keep) her prisoner, but ______________________ (treat) her well. She ______________________ (live) in Jamestown as a prisoner for a few months when she ______________________ (decide) to get baptised[2] and to marry a settler called John Rolf. This marriage ______________________ (stop) the war between the Europeans and the Indians that ______________________ (go) on for almost a year. Some time later, after she ______________________ (have) a baby, whom she ______________________ (name) Thomas, she ______________________ (travel) to England with her husband. Unfortunately though, Rebecca (which was now her name) ______________________ (die) in England after she ______________________ (become) ill. She was only 22 years old, but she ______________________ (do) a lot to bring the two peoples[3] together.

1 **ransom** – Lösegeld; 2 **to baptise** – taufen; 3 **peoples** – *hier:* Völker

one point for each gap — *points:* 16

0–10 points ☹	11–15 points 😐	16–21 points ☺
You've made quite a lot of mistakes – you should read this chapter again!	That was OK, but you can do better!	You did a really good job!

maximum number of points: 21

2 Conditional sentences

1 Check-up

Which type of conditional sentences are these?

	I	II	III
What would you do if you saw a black bear?		x	
If I saw a black bear, I would stay calm and think, "Wow, this is really cool!"			
If you meet a bear, there are several things that might happen.			
If the bear sees you, it will usually leave, because it doesn't care much about people.			
Bears sometimes start running towards you if they feel threatened.			
If this happens, just talk softly to the bear and walk slowly backwards.			
Never run away! Many accidents would not have happened if people hadn't run away from a bear.			

Bedingungssätze

Im Englischen gibt es drei Typen von Bedingungssätzen. Sie unterscheiden sich durch die **Wahrscheinlichkeit**, mit der die Bedingung, die im Bedingungssatz *(if-clause)* genannt wird, eintritt.

Typ I	**Typ II**	**Typ III**
wahrscheinlich	eher unwahrscheinlich	absolut unmöglich, da die Bedingung in der Vergangenheit formuliert ist (Was wäre gewesen, wenn …? oder: Was hätte sein können, wenn …?).
If you **meet** a bear, there are several things that **might happen**.	What **would you do** if you **saw** a black bear?	Many accidents **would not have happened**, if people **hadn't run** away from a bear.

Je nach Typ ändern sich auch die Zeiten der Verben in Haupt- und Nebensatz.

Typ	**Hauptsatz**	**Nebensatz (*if-clause*)**
I	*will future* oder modales Hilfsverb + Infinitiv oder Imperativ	*present tense*
II	*conditional I* oder *could* (könnte) + Infinitiv oder *might* (würde vielleicht) + Infinitiv	*past tense*
III	*conditional II* (*would have + past participle / could have + past participle / might have + past participle*)	*past perfect* (*had + past participle*)

Achtung:
Im *if*-Satz steht nie das *conditional*, also nie *would*.
Das Komma steht nur, wenn der *if*-Satz am Anfang steht.

2.1 Conditional sentences type I

2

The underlined parts of these sentences have been mixed up. Find out which parts belong together, and rewrite them.

Rules and Regulations in Death Valley National Park

1. If we want Death Valley to remain a nice, safe and clean place, please see the Rangers at Furnace Creek Visitor Center and ask them about campsites.
2. Animal and plant life will be damaged if you feed them.
3. If you own a gun, every visitor must follow some rules.
4. Please use the fire pits* in the official campgrounds if you leave the roads with your car or motorcycle.
5. If you are planning to camp in the park, we ask you kindly not to bring it. Hunting is strictly forbidden.
6. Wild animals might become ill or even die if you want to make a fire.

***fire pit** – Feuerstelle

3

Conditional sentences type I. Translate the following sentences.

1. Wenn Sie die Regeln brechen, müssen Sie Strafe[1] bezahlen.

   ____

2. Wenn zu viele Menschen die Regeln brechen, werden sie verschärft[2].

   ____

3. Bitte seien Sie besonders vorsichtig, wenn Sie mit Kindern reisen.

   ____

1 Strafe – **a fine**; 2 verschärfen – **to make s.th. stricter, more severe**

2.2 Conditional sentences type II

4

What would the people do if things were different?

At a campground in Yosemite National Park

John: 	Melissa: 	Abigail: 
climb El Capitano	go hiking	drive home today
Mike: 	Martha: 	Kyle: 
drink some water	watch the sunset	go biking

Example: *If John's arm wasn't broken, he would climb El Capitano.*

5

Translate the following sentences.

1. Wenn ich ein Zelt hätte, würde ich in der Wildnis* schlafen.

____

2. Wenn ich in der Wildnis schlafen würde, würde ich viele Tiere sehen.

____

3. Ich würde mich sehr freuen, wenn ich einen Bär sehen würde.

____

*Wildnis – **wilderness**

2.3 Conditional sentences type III

6

Read the story, then finish the sentences below.

When I met a bear

In 1995 I was working for a large oil company, and I had to do some work for them in the wilderness. The weather had been terrible for days and so the road – which was really bad anyway – was very muddy. That's why my truck got stuck. I got out of the truck and tried to get it moving again. That was when I saw a black bear cub[1]. How cute, I thought, but then I saw its mother. Mama-bear was not at all happy to see me, though – and I don't think she thought that I was cute, either. She charged[2] at me right away. I was very afraid and wanted to run away. I couldn't, though, because I was stuck in the mud – and that probably saved my life. The bear ran towards me, but stopped right in front of me. Then it roared[3] right in my face, so close that I could smell its breath. I can remember saying something stupid like, "Please don't eat me. I'm a really nice guy." Then the bear left – but I had nightmares for about three weeks.

1 **cub** – baby bear; 2 **to charge** – to run towards someone in order to attack him/her;
3 **to roar** – to scream

Everything could have been different

Example:
If the weather hadn't been terrible for days, (road / not be / so muddy)
If the weather hadn't been terrible for days, the road would not have been so muddy.

1. The truck wouldn't have got stuck if (the road / not be / so muddy)

____

____

2. If the truck hadn't got stuck, (he / stay / inside it)

____

____

3. He might not have seen the cub if (he / not get out of / the car)

4. If he hadn't got out of the car, (mama-bear / might not see / him)

5. If she hadn't seen him, (she / not charge / at him)

6. He would have run away if (he / not be stuck / in the mud)

7. He might have been killed if (he / run / away)

8. If the bear hadn't roared right in his face, (he / not smell / its breath)

9. He would not have had nightmares for weeks if (all this / not happen)

7

Rewrite the sentences below using Type III if-clauses.
Be careful: positive sentences must be turned into negative sentences, and vice versa!

Great lies about bear encounters[1]

Example:
The bear walked away because I had given it my hamburger.
The bear wouldn't have walked away if I hadn't given it my hamburger.

1. The two cubs played soccer with me because I had a ball.

___

___

___

2. The bear didn't kill me because I started singing a lullaby[2].

___

___

___

3. The bear didn't see me because it had lost its glasses.

___

___

___

4. I was able to kill the bear because I had brought my pocket knife.

___

___

___

1 encounter – Begegnung; **2 lullaby** – Schlaflied

5. The bear started singing when I gave it a glass of whisky.

____

____

____

6. The bear ran away from me because I hadn't taken a shower for a week.

____

____

____

8

Translate the following sentences.

1. Wenn ich einen Bären gesehen hätte, hätte ich Angst bekommen.

____

____

2. Der Bär hätte möglicherweise angegriffen, wenn er gemerkt hätte, dass ich Angst hatte.

____

____

3. Wenn er angegriffen hätte, wäre ich davongelaufen.

____

____

4. Wenn ich davongelaufen wäre, hätte er mich möglicherweise getötet.

____

____

2.4 Conditional sentences type I, II or III?

9

Match the sentence parts from the two boxes to make complete sentences. The tenses will help you to decide which sentence goes with which.

A trip to Yosemite

A group of teenagers went on a trip to Yosemite. Here are things they said to each other before, during and after their trip.

If we go hiking in Yosemite …
If we had taken a map with us, …
Alex would come with us to Yosemite …
If Alex hadn't been so lazy throughout the school year, …
We will rent a tent …
I would climb El Capitano …
If we had got up earlier …
If we don't pitch* the tent soon …
We wouldn't have gotten so wet …
If we caught a fish, …

… we wouldn't have lost the way.
… if I was a better climber.
… if he didn't have to go to summer school.
… we will see a lot of animals.
… he could have come with us to Yosemite.
… I would cook it for dinner.
… we could have seen the beautiful sunrise.
… if we had pitched the tent sooner.
… we will get very wet.
… if we go on an overnight trip.

***to pitch** – aufschlagen

–

–

–

–

–

–

–

–

–

–

10 2

Fill in the gaps using the correct forms of the verbs in brackets. You can listen to the CD to check your answers.

In the evening before they go to bed, they have to discuss their day and their plans for the rest of the trip.

Jenny: If we ______________________ **(walk)** tomorrow as far as we did today, I ______________________ **(die)**.

Andrea: I agree, Jenny – but it ______________________ **(be)** so bad if Bill ______________________ **(not lose)** the map.

Bill: That's not fair! If you ______________________ **(put)** it in my backpack after the break, I ______________________ **(not lose)** it.

John: You know, I think we should worry about the weather. If it ______________________ **(not rain)**, we ______________________ **(sit)** outside now and watch the stars.

Andrea: Oh John, you're so romantic. If we ______________________ **(have)** you with us, we ______________________ **(forget)** about the beauty of nature altogether.

John: That's right. And if you ______________________ **(not be)** here, nobody ______________________ **(make)** smart comments all the time.

Jenny: Well, if I ever ______________________ **(return)** home, I ______________________ **(take)** a long, hot bath and afterwards I ______________________ **(look)** at the stars – if it ______________________ **(not rain)**, of course.

John: Ha, ha. If I ______________________ **(survive)** this trip, I ______________________ **(write)** a book about it.

1

Cross out the incorrect verb forms in these sentences. Sometimes more than one option is correct.

1. If you want to take a rafting trip through the Grand Canyon, you **must take / had had to take / had to take** a bus ride to Diamond Creek.
2. Groups of teenagers will only be admitted if they **bring / will bring / might bring** an adult.
3. If people **don't fall / didn't fall / won't fall** into the water very often on these trips, they wouldn't be so popular.
4. If people aren't careful, they **will be hurt / might be hurt / had been hurt**.
5. "If I **didn't go / hadn't gone / wouldn't have gone**, I would have regretted it afterwards," one guest said last week.
6. If more people **went on / go on / might go on** this trip, they would understand how beautiful the world is.
7. People **wouldn't treat / might not treat / will not treat** the environment as badly if they realized how beautiful the world is.

one point for each sentence points: 7

2

Fill in the gaps using the verbs from the box.

be (3x)	not bring	buy	not spend
travel	pack	break	not take

If you ______________________ from one National Park to the next, you have to plan your trip carefully. You have to make sure that your car is in good shape. If it ______________________ down somewhere in the desert between two parks, it ______________________ difficult to get help quickly. It ______________________ also important to take enough water with you if you drive through the deserts of Nevada. A friend of mine told me recently: "If I ______________________ extra water with me last summer, I'd be dead now." He had been stuck in the desert with a flat tire for two days.

You should also take a good tent and a warm sleeping bag with you. "If only the nights weren't so cold, travelling the National Parks ______________________ much more comfortable," my husband said when we woke up and found frozen puddles in front of our tent in Montana. "Well," I answered, "if you ______________________ yourself a good sleeping bag, you wouldn't mind so much." He was quite mad at me then and said: "I would have bought a better sleeping bag if you ______________________ all our money on the camping stove* – and if you don't get out of your beautifully warm sleeping bag right now and make some coffee, I ______________________ my bags and go home." So the end of the story is: if I ______________________ the coffee, my vacation would have been over right then."

***stove** – Campingkocher

points: 10 *one point for each gap*

3

Make conditional sentences.

1. America / not have / so many National Parks / not so many people / go there / on vacation

2. people / like / the National Parks / they / protect / the environment more actively

3. I / not enjoyed / my last vacation / I / not visit / the Grand Canyon

one point for each sentence

points: 3

0 – 7 points ☹	8 – 13 points 😐	14 – 20 points ☺
You've made quite a lot of mistakes – you should read this chapter again!	That was OK, but you can do better!	You did a really good job!

maximum number of points: 20

3 Relative clauses

3.1 Defining relative clauses

1 Check-up

Explain the underlined words, using the information from the table to form relative clauses.

Sandra is an exchange student from Germany, and she's just arrived in Bismarck (North Dakota, USA). On her first day at Bismarck High School she is standing in front of the bulletin board, but she doesn't understand all the words there. Another pupil explains them to her.

First football try-out on Wednesday at 2:30.

Yearbook team!
Are you ready for our annual task?
Let's do it again this year.
Friday, 6th period.

Cheerleaders!
This is our year!
We'll win the championship!
Come to practice today at 3 p.m.!
GO Wolverines!!!!!

Choir members. Please bring last year's notes to first rehearsal on Tuesday!

are a group of girls is a group of boys is a group of students (2x) is something is an animal is a kind of practice (2x)	that which who	helps to find out who the best players are. sing together. lives in the woods, but it's also our school's mascot. try to help our sports teams during the games. performers do to learn their parts. write a book about the school year. must be done.

Example:

A try-out is a kind of practice that helps to find out who the best players are.

Cheerleaders ______________________________

____

____

A Wolverine ______________________________

____

____

The Yearbook team ______________________________

____

____

A task ______________________________

____

____

A choir ______________________________

____

____

A rehearsal ______________________________

____

____

Relativsätze

Relativsätze (*relative clauses*) sind Nebensätze, die eine Person, eine Sache oder eine Situation näher beschreiben.

Cheerleaders are a group of girls **who try to help our sports teams during the games**.

Nur durch den Relativsatz wissen wir, was Cheerleader wirklich sind, ohne ihn wüssten wir lediglich, dass sie eine Gruppe von Mädchen sind:

Cheerleaders are a group of girls.

Relativpronomen

Es ist wichtig, das richtige **Relativpronomen** zu verwenden.

Für Personen	Für Dinge und Tiere
who / that whom (formelles Englisch in der Objektform)	which / that

Im formellen Englisch gibt es noch das besitzanzeigende Relativpronomen ***whose***.

These are the players **whose team won the championship last year**.

Verkürzen von Relativsätzen *(contact clauses)*

Wenn das Relativpronomen Objekt des Relativsatzes ist, kann man es im gesprochenen und informellen geschriebenen Englisch auch weglassen.

Relativsatz	contact clause
The wolverine **which / that I saw yesterday** had a bloody mouth.	The wolverine **I saw yesterday** had a bloody mouth.

2

Fill in the gaps using the correct relative pronoun(s).

who / which / that / whose

During Sandra's first week at Bismarck High School, her class worked on a project about youth culture. Each group had to present a worksheet and a questionnaire at the end of the project. Here they are.

Pocket money

How much pocket money should a teenager get ____________ is 16 years old and still living at home? Parents ____________ earn a lot of money often don't think enough about this question, and give their kids as much as they ask for. Their children are the ones ____________ come to school with expensive new electronic devices ____________ they have bought "just like that" on their way to school. In contrast, the parents ____________ children have very little money are often the ones ____________ think that they are behaving more responsibly. They think that children ____________ still go to school are too young to make important decisions about money, and should learn to live with just a little bit of money. But of course the kids ____________ do not have a lot of pocket money have serious problems, because they have to compete with their classmates ____________ pockets are stuffed with money. We believe that pocket money is one of the reasons ____________ make life difficult for many of us.

What do you think about pocket money? Tick your answer![1]

	agree	don't agree
Only students ___________ get at least $20 a week should be allowed to come to Bismarck High.		
The student government should decide on the amount of money ___________ students are allowed to bring to school.		
A student's pocket money and what he or she does with it is not a matter ___________ the school should be interested in.		
The principal[2] should talk to the parents ___________ give their children too much money.		

1 Wenn du möchtest, kannst du hier und bei allen anderen Fragebögen natürlich deine persönliche Antwort eintragen. **2 principal (AE)** – American title for a school's headmaster

3

Where it's possible, make contact clauses by crossing out the relative pronoun.

Should teenagers work for their money?

We have interviewed people who we met in the streets and collected their opinions. Here they are:

Older lady: I believe that teenagers **who work for their money** don't have enough time to work for school. I also believe that parents **whose children work** are not responsible parents.

Little boy: My brother works at the ice-cream parlor* downtown. I think that was the best idea **that he ever had** because I always get ice-cream for free.

Owner of ice-cream parlor: Teenagers are good cheap workers. The amount of ice-cream **that I have sold since I started employing teenagers** has risen quite a bit. But the number of friends **who they give the ice-cream for free** is also quite large.

Mother of two teenagers: Working with your own two hands is one of the experiences **which every person should make sooner or later**. I believe that money **that was earned by hard work** will be spent responsibly. Both of my children work.

School teacher: Teenagers **who have never had a job during their school time** miss an important experience. However, the teenagers' most important job is school. Jobs **that keep students from doing their homework** should be forbidden by responsible parents.

***ice cream parlor (AE)** – Eisdiele

What's your opinion on teenage work?

	that's right	no way
Teenagers **who get bad marks at school** should ask their teacher before they start a job.		
Parents **who allow their kids to work at nights** should be punished.		
Jobs **that the teenagers do to help the family to pay for food and rent** are absolutely OK, even if the kids get bad marks.		
It must be the teenagers themselves **who decide if they want to work or not**. It's nobody else's business.		

3.2 Non-defining relative clauses

4 Check-up

Look at the sentences below. Are the relative clauses important for an understanding of what is being said, or do they give extra information that could be left out? Mark the correct answer. The letters of the solution spell out an important part of a non-defining relative clause (*ergänzender Relativsatz*).

	important	extra information
Mr. Cohen, who is eighty years old, thinks that today's teenagers watch too much TV.	u	c
Philip thinks that TV shows that teach teenagers something are very helpful.	o	i
Many people believe that the internet, which is used by millions of people every day, has been one of the greatest inventions of the last century.	n	m
MP3 players can contain a lot more music than a disc-man could, which is very useful if you are away from home for a long time.	d	m
A digital camera is a camera that takes photos without needing a film.	a	g

Solution:

A very important part of a non-defining relative clause is

the ______________________________ .

Ergänzende Relativsätze

Ergänzende Relativsätze liefern Informationen, die ergänzen oder ausschmücken. Diese Informationen sind für das Verständnis des Satzes an sich nicht notwendig. Man nennt sie deshalb *non-defining relative clauses*: Sie definieren das Subjekt nicht bzw. bestimmen es nicht näher.

Lies die Sätze mit den ergänzenden Relativsätzen aus dem Check-up noch einmal durch und decke dabei die Relativsätze ab. Du wirst sehen, dass der Inhalt auch ohne sie gut zu verstehen ist.

> Mr. Cohen**, who is eighty years old,** thinks that today's teenagers watch too much TV.
> Mr. Cohen thinks that today's teenagers watch too much TV.

Lässt du dagegen einen bestimmenden Relativsatz (*defining relative clause*) weg, verliert der Satz seinen Sinn:

> Philip thinks that TV shows **that teach teenagers something** are very helpful.
> Philip thinks that TV shows are very helpful.

Durch das Weglassen des Relativsatzes wird Philips Meinung verfälscht: nicht alle TV-Sendungen sind hilfreich.

Bestimmender Relativsatz *(Defining relative clause)*	**Ergänzender Relativsatz** *(Non-defining relative clause)*
kein Komma zwischen Hauptsatz und Relativsatz	Relativsatz vom Hauptsatz durch Kommas abgetrennt
that und *which* als Relativpronomen für Dinge möglich	nur *which* als Relativpronomen für Dinge möglich
Relativpronomen kann im *contact clause* weggelassen werden	Relativpronomen kann nie weggelassen werden
Für Personen im Objekt *who / that* oder *whom*	Für Personen im Objekt und nach Präpositionen steht *whom*

Satzbezügliches *which*

which kann auch einen Relativsatz einleiten, der sich auf einen ganzen Satz bezieht. Man benutzt es gerne, um Kommentare abzugeben:

> MP3 players can contain a lot more music than a disc-man could, **which is very useful if you are away from home for a long time.**

5

Do these sentences contain a defining relative clause (def.) or a non-defining relative clause with extra information (extra)? Tick the correct answer and add commas where necessary.

Other classes at Bismarck High School worked on the project, too. Here are some of their results.

Internet addiction[1]

	def.	extra
Using the internet is a hobby that may cost families a lot of money.		
Especially if the teenagers spend a lot of time on pay sites which are usually made to trick their users anyway.		
Many of theses pay sites which make their owners rich and their users poor are gaming sites.		
The real problems arise when teenagers whose parents often find out too late about their hobby become addicted[2] to their game.		
Even if their parents take their computers away from them it doesn't change anything for the teenagers who then just go to internet cafes to go online.		
Psychologists say that internet-addiction is a problem that is almost as serious as drug-addiction.		
However, they say that there are at least as many internet-addicts among grown-ups as among teenagers which is not really surprising because they have enough money to finance it.		
For those addicts who want to solve the problem it is important to accept that there is a problem.		
Once they have done that, they can look for a psychiatrist who is specialised in internet addiction.		

1 **addiction** – Abhängigkeit/Sucht; 2 **addicted** – süchtig

6

The second sentences below contain extra information – add this information to the first sentences using non-defining clauses.

A daydream (short story)

Example:
Marc spends five hours in front of his TV every day.
He is 12 years old.
Marc, who is 12 years old, spends five hours in front of his TV every day.

1. His father thinks that this is normal for a teenager.
   He works for a TV company.

   ____

   ____

2. His mother believes that Marc watches too much TV.
   She is a housewife.

   ____

   ____

3. She has talked to other parents from Marc's school and they all agreed with her.
   Its name is Glenwood Springs High School.

   ____

   ____

4. She also tried to tell him to go and spend more time outside with his friends.
   They play a lot of soccer.

   ____

   ____

5. But Marc told her that he didn't have any friends and that he would much rather keep on watching his favourite show.
   It is called "The Simpsons".

   ____

   ____

6. When she heard this she started to cry and screamed at Marc.
   He just sat there and didn't understand what her problem was.

   ____

   ____

7. At that moment she woke up from her nap* and saw Marc walking out of the house with his tennis-racket in his hand.
   She had taken the nap in the garden.

   ____

   ____

*nap – Mittagsschlaf

7

Decide which "which" it is: does it refer to a word from the main clause, or does it refer to a whole sentence? Add commas where necessary.

Another daydream

	word	sentence
Our school has a new computer lab which was installed this summer.		
The teachers are now looking for a group of pupils which want to look after the room during the breaks.		
My best friend wants to join the group which is really good for me, because then he can show me everything.		
You know, I'm really bad with computers which is something I want to change.		
If he helps me, I will soon be able to join the computer club which is the coolest club at school.		
That's because the members of the computer club can always help other students with their computer problems which makes them very popular.		

8

Look at the comments below: add these to the sentences, using "which".

This shows that many people are still copying music illegally.

This is an easy way to earn money.

That's quite understandable.

This has of course not made everybody happy.

This is usually illegal.

This shows that the laws might be quite successful.

Example:
Many people download the music they listen to from the internet,
which is usually illegal.

Internet crime

1. Others copy thousands of CDs and sell them.

   ____

2. The companies who sell the music are of course angry with these people.

   ____

3. Finally, more and more governments have passed laws punishing such behaviour.

   ____

4. The people who have illegally copied music are afraid of going to jail.

   ____

5. Yet most music companies think that the punishments should be much greater.

   ____

1

Fill in the gaps using the correct relative pronoun. Put in commas where necessary.

If you're designing a website ___________ is aimed at teenagers, you'd better not make the fonts* too small. That's not because teens have bad eyes, but because teenagers ___________ sit in front of their computers tend to lean back in their chairs.

This advice and much more for people ___________ want to create websites for teens can be found in a new book by Jakob Nielsen. Since three quarters of all American teens are web users, people ___________ job it is to get teenagers to use the internet should be very interested in this book ___________ is already a bestseller.

"It's interactivity ___________ makes the difference. That's what all teenagers are looking for," says Nielsen ___________ prepared for the study by observing American and Australian teenagers using dozens of websites. They want to be doing something, "as opposed to just sitting and reading ___________ they think is boring. Apart from that, they say that reading is something ___________ they do enough of already in school." The best interactive elements include message boards, polls, quizzes, being able to ask questions of experts, and tools ___________ let teens construct their own web pages.

Another element teens find attractive is the use of photographs and images ___________ make texts easier to understand. Teens are much less willing than adults to spend time on websites ___________ have a lot of good information but are no fun to look at." Adults ___________ might need the information for their work are more willing to read long texts without pictures or animations.

*font – *hier:* Schrift

points: 18 *one point for every relative pronoun and one for every comma*

2

Underline all the relative clauses and rewrite them making contact clauses if possible.

In his book Nielsen names some sites that teenagers like. One is *SparkNotes*, which offers study guides on subjects from math to chemistry. He explains that the teens who took part in his study enjoyed the site's combination of useful information, good design and interactivity. The other part of the site which they liked was its interface, which made it easy for them to find what they needed to do their homework.

CSUMentor and *TeensHealth* were other sites which the teenagers liked because they smartly mix information and presentation and don't ask teens to work too hard, which seems to show that teens who surf the net might be just a little bit lazy.

____

____

____

____

____

____

____

____

one point for every underlining and one for every contact clause

points: 10

0–15 points ☹	16–23 points 😐	24–28 points ☺
You've made quite a lot of mistakes – you should read this chapter again!	That was OK, but you can do better!	You did a really good job!

maximum number of points: 28

4 Talking about the future

1 Check-up

The Adams family are talking about the future. Which tense is used in each sentence? Number the tenses correctly!

(1.) simple present (2.) present progressive
(3.) *going to*-future (4.) *will*-future

◯ Mr. and Mrs. Schuster and their twins Kai and Sophie are going to visit us this summer.

◯ I believe you will like their children a lot.

◯ That's not a good idea. I'm visiting friends in Montana this summer.

◯ Summer vacation starts on July 26th.

Mr. Adams Mrs. Adams Jennifer Ken

◯ Mrs. Schuster is also a teacher, so she is going to visit our school.

◯ Don't worry, Jennifer. Their plane back to Germany leaves on July 6th.

◯ They won't interfere with your trip to Montana.

◯ Great! We'll show them Chicago.

◯ I'll get some brochures for tourists.

1 **interfere** – *hier:* überschneiden, dazwischenkommen

Über die Zukunft sprechen

Das Englische verfügt über mehrere Formen, um Ereignisse in der Zukunft auszudrücken. Dabei sagt jede Form etwas anderes über die zukünftigen Ereignisse aus.

Das *going to*-Futur

Bildung

	to be (am/are/is)	+	**going to**	+	Verb im Infinitiv	
Mrs. Schuster	**is**		**going to**		**visit**	our school.

Der Bestandteil *going to* bleibt **immer** unverändert.
Für Fragen wird, wie bei anderen zusammengesetzten Prädikaten auch, nur das Hilfsverb, also die Form von *to be*, vor das Subjekt gesetzt:

Is Mrs. Schuster **going to visit** our school?

Auch die Verneinung wird beim Hilfsverb vorgenommen.

Mrs. Schuster **is not/isn't going to visit** our school.

Verwendung
Das *going to*-Futur wird verwendet, um

- **Pläne** oder **Absichten** für die Zukunft zu äußern:
  The Schusters are going to visit us this summer.
- Für **Vorhersagen** aufgrund von deutlich sichtbaren **Anzeichen**:
  From the look on Jenny's face I can tell that we are going to have a lot of fun.

Das *will*-Futur

Bildung

	will / 'll	+	Infinitiv	
I believe that **you**	**will / you'll**		**like**	them a lot.

Will wird nicht verändert. Die Kurzform von *will* ist *'ll*.

Fragen werden durch das Umstellen des Hilfsverbs *will* vor das Subjekt gebildet:

Will they love Chicago?

Bei Verneinungen wird außer der eher seltenen Vollform *will not* vor allem die zusammengezogene Form *won't* verwendet.

We **will not / won't** enjoy the heat of the city.

Verwendung
Das *will*-Futur wird verwendet für

- **Vorhersagen** und **Vermutungen**, über die der Sprecher in der Regel keine Kontrolle hat.

  I believe that you'll like them a lot.

- die Äußerung eines **spontanen Entschlusses**:

  Great! We'll show them Chicago. I'll get some brochures for tourists.

Present progressive und *simple present*

1. *Present progressive:*

   I'm visiting friends in Montana in the summer.

2. *Simple present*:

   Their plane back to Germany **leaves** on July 6th.

Verwendung des *present progressive* zum Ausdruck der Zukunft
Der Sprecher drückt damit aus, dass es sich um einen persönlichen Plan oder eine Absprache handelt, die bereits fest vereinbart ist. Der Unterschied zum *going to-future* besteht darin, dass die Ereignisse bereits viel verbindlicher geplant sind (siehe der erste Satz oben.)

Verwendung des *simple present* zum Ausdruck der Zukunft
Der Sprecher verweist damit auf zukünftige Ereignisse, die - meist offiziell - so festgelegt sind, dass sie schon als Tatsachen betrachtet werden. Sie liegen dann in der Regel schon in gedruckter Form vor, wie z. B. Ferienbeginn, Abfahrts- und Ankunftszeiten von Flugzeugen, Zügen, Bussen oder Veranstaltungsprogramme. Man spricht deshalb auch vom *timetable-future* (siehe der zweite Satz oben).
Die Wahl der falschen Futurform kann also durchaus zu Missverständnissen führen!

4.1 The *going to*-future

2 (CD) 3

Fill in the correct form of the *going to*-future. You can listen to the CD to check your answers.

1. *Ken:* Well, Mum and Dad, we've actually worked out a really good plan. First, we ______________________ **(take)** Kai and Sophie to Sears Tower Skydeck to give them a view over the city. We ______________________ **(not do)** a guided tour of Chicago, though. We both think that's boring. Instead Kai and Sophie ______________________________ **(experience)** Chicago together with us.

2. *Jennifer:* I ______________________ **(show)** them the most interesting places and Ken ______________________ **(explain)** baseball to them. We ______________________ ____________ **(also watch)** a game.

3. *Mr. Adams:* Which team ______________________________ **(watch)**, the Cubs or the White Sox?

4. *Ken:* The Chicago White Sox, of course. They __________________ ________________ **(get to know)** a real team, not just losers!

5. *Jennifer:* I am ______________________ **(go)** to Navy Pier with them. And we ______________________________ **(have a look at)** the sharks at the Shedd Aquarium.

Ken: Those are our ideas so far.

Mr. Adams: That sounds good.

4.2 The *will*-future

3 4

Fill in the gaps using the *will*-future form of the verbs from the box. You can listen to the CD to check your answers.

be **enjoy** **say** **find**
not survive **need to add** **prefer**

Is this what the Schusters will want to do in Chicago?

1. *Mrs. Adams:* But don't you think that the weather ______________ great for a boat tour on the Chicago River?
2. *Jennifer:* I guess Sophie ______________ to go shopping. That's more interesting.
3. *Ken:* I'm sure that we ______________ something interesting for everybody.
4. *Mr. Adams:* We just hope you ______________ all ______________ yourselves. You don't need to show them everything. Just have fun.
5. *Mrs. Adams:* But they should do something more than just shopping and baseball. What ______________ their parents ______________ if their children get the impression that Chicago is just a big shopping mall?
6. *Mr. Adams:* Not to forget all the baseball! You heard it children. You ______________ some more cultural highlights.
7. *Jennifer:* The chance that I ______________ this visit has just reached 80 per cent.

4.3 Mixed future tenses

4 5

Fill in the gaps using the *going to*-future or the *will*-future. You can listen to the CD to check your answers.

The Schusters have arrived now. Jennifer and Ken are talking to Sophie and Kai.

1. *Ken:* So what ______________________ **(you do)** on your first day here?
2. *Kai:* I ______________________ **(sleep)** a lot. I'm so tired.
3. *Sophie:* I ______________________ **(unpack)** my suitcase. But I think I ______________________ **(have to help)** my mother do some shopping, too.
4. *Jennifer:* That's just like in our family. I also have to do the shopping for my lazy brother. I ______________________ **(help)** you, Sophie.
5. *Ken:* Thanks, Jenny. You're so charming. I think I ______________________ **(help)** Mum and Dad. It looks as if we ______________________ **(have)** a barbecue this evening. Well, the weather is great for it.
6. *Jennifer:* I guess Leslie and Brian ______________________ **(not be)** around tonight. But Antonio is here. Could you give him a call?
7. *Ken:* No problem. I ______________________ **(call)** him. Perhaps he can come.

5

Simple present or present progressive?
Using the information in the pictures and the verbs written under them, write future tense sentences using the simple present or the present progressive.

Jennifer and Ken are showing Sophie and Kai around Chicago.

1. boat tour / to start

2. Brian and Leslie / to meet / us / Sears Tower

3. you / to stay / how long?

4. museum / to close

5. to take / bus

6. bus / to leave

Example:

1. *Ken: The boat tour starts at 10:30.*
2. *Jennifer:* ____________________
3. *Brian:* ____________________
4. *Sophie:* ____________________
5. *Jennifer:* ____________________
6. *Ken:* ____________________

6 CD 6

Will-future, *going to*-future or simple present?
Fill in the gaps using the *will*-future, *going to*-future or *simple present*-future forms of the verbs in brackets.
You can listen to the CD to check your answers.

It is evening now, and the children have finished their tour of Chicago:

1. *Ken:* Oh no, it's 8:25 already … We ____________________ **(probably miss)** the bus that ____________________ **(leave)** at 8:30 from the station, and we ____________________ **(to be late)** for dinner. Mom ____________________ **(be happy)** about that.
2. *Jennifer:* Let's check when the other buses ____________________ **(to run)**. Who's got the plan ?
3. *Brian:* I've got it. Let's see. Number six ____________________ **(leave)** at 8:35. Do you think ____________________ **(be able to)** make that?
4. *Sophie:* Don't worry, I ____________________ **(run)** the Berlin Marathon in September. I can run for quite a while.
5. *Leslie:* You ____________________ **(take part)** in a marathon? Cool!
6. *Brian:* Well, then, let's run and let's see who ____________________ **(be)** first …

1 7

Fill in the gaps using the *going to*-future forms of the verbs in brackets. You can listen to the CD to check your answers.

A week has passed, and now it's time to say good bye.

1. *Ken:* ______________________ **(you really fly)** to the West Coast tomorrow? That's sad.
2. *Kai:* Yes. But we don't want to. We ______________________ **(not go)**. Sophie and I have changed our plans. We want to stay here.
3. *Sophie:* And how ______________________ **(convince)** our parents?
4. *Kai:* I ______________________ **(just tell)** them to pick us up here in Chicago on their way back to Germany.
5. *Jennifer:* Good idea. Our parents really like you. I'm sure they ______________________ **(let you stay)** here for two more weeks.

points: *one point for every gap*

2 8

Fill in the gaps using the *will*-future form of the verbs in brackets. You can listen to the CD to check your answers.

1. *Jennifer:* I ______________________ **(miss)** you, Sophie.
2. *Sophie:* Can't we stay for two more weeks, mum? The rest of our trip ______________________ **(not be)** as good as Chicago anyway.
3. *Kai:* Yes, why don't you leave us here and pick us up on the way back? We ______________________ **(help)** Mr. and Mrs. Adams in the house.
4. *Mrs. Schuster:* No, I'm sorry children. That's not possible. But perhaps the Adams family ______________________ **(come)** to Germany one day.
5. *Mrs. Adams:* That sounds great. We ______________________ **(think)** about it.

points: *one point for every gap*

3 9

Fill in the gaps using the *going to*-future, *will*-future, *simple present* or *present progressive* forms of the verbs in brackets. You can listen to the CD to check your answers.

Can Jennifer and Ken really go to Germany?

1. *Jennifer:* Oh mom, please. Let us visit them in Germany. It ______________ **(be)** so much fun.
2. *Mrs. Adams:* Well, it's not that easy. We ______________________ **(have to think)** about a lot of things before we can make such a big decision.
3. *Mr. Adams:* For example, who __________________________ **(mess up)** your room when you're away, Jen? I mean, somebody has to do it.

   Jennifer: Dad! I'm serious.
4. *Mrs. Adams:* Well, one important point is the summer vacation. When ______________________________ **(it start)** in Germany next year?
5. *Mrs. Schuster:* I'm not quite sure. Sometime at the beginning of August. Wait a second, I ______________________ **(look it up)**. It's August 3rd.
6. *Mrs. Adams:* Well, we ______________________________ **(have)** a big family meeting in Boston the week before, but after that it's all right.
7. *Jennifer:* Really, mom? That's fantastic. I ______________________________ **(really go)** to Germany.
8. *Sophie:* And we __________________ **(show)** you Munich. You ______________________ **(see)** the German Museum, the English Garden and …

one point for every gap

points: 9

0–10 points ☹	11–15 points 😐	16–19 points ☺
You've made quite a lot of mistakes – you should read this chapter again!	That was OK, but you can do better!	You did a really good job!

maximum number of points: 19

5 Modal auxiliaries and their replacements

1 Check-up

Tick the correct answer.

At school

Which question is more polite[1]?

☐ May I go to the bathroom? ☐ Can I go to the bathroom?

Which teacher is more serious?

☐ You can't talk in class! ☐ You mustn't talk in class!

Which student is more sure about what he can see?

☐ The man in the picture could be an Indian. ☐ The man in the picture might be an Indian.

In which sentence does the teacher tell the students that the homework is not really important?

☐ You needn't do this homework. ☐ You shouldn't do this homework.

You want to tell your friends that you can't come to the party because your parents don't want you to. What do you say?

☐ I'm not able to come to the party tonight. ☐ I'm not allowed to come to the party tonight.

How do you say "I must do my homework" using the simple past?

☐ I must do my homework. ☐ I had to do my homework.

How do you say "I can't go to school because I'm ill" using the *will*-future?

☐ I will can't go to school because I'm ill. ☐ I won't be able to go to school because I'm ill.

1 **polite** – höflich

Modale Hilfsverben und ihre Ersatzformen

Modale Hilfsverben verfeinern die Sprache. Verwechselt man sie jedoch, kann man unter Umständen ganz schön ins Fettnäpfchen treten.
Sie werden zum Beispiel verwendet, um zu sagen, was man **kann**, was **wichtig** oder **unwichtig** ist oder auch was jemand machen **muss** oder **soll**. Außerdem kann man mit ihnen ausdrücken, ob etwas **wahrscheinlich** oder **möglich** ist. Schließlich sind sie sehr wichtig, wenn es um **Höflichkeit** geht.

Übersicht wichtiger modaler Hilfsverben und ihrer Verneinungen

can	can't	können / dürfen
could	could not / couldn't	könnte
must / have to	need not / needn't / don't have to	müssen / nicht brauchen
may	may not / mustn't	dürfen
might	might not / mustn't	dürfen
shall	shall not	sollen
should	should not / shouldn't	sollte
ought to	ought not to	sollen (mehr moralisch gemeint)
need	need not / needn't	brauchen

Für alle Hilfsverben gelten folgende Regeln:

1. Auf ein modales Hilfsverb folgt immer ein Infinitiv ohne *to*.
   I must **do** my homework now.
2. Modale Hilfsverben haben kein „s" in der 3. Person Singular:
   The man in the picture **could** be an Indian.
3. Modale Hilfsverben werden ohne ***to do*** verneint und bilden Fragen ohne to do:
   You **shouldn't** do this homework. **May** I go to the bathroom?
4. Modale Hilfsverben bilden nicht alle Zeitformen. Deshalb gibt es verschiedene Ersatzformen.
   I **can** come to school when my headache is gone.
   I **will be able to** come to school when my headache is gone.

Übersicht der Ersatzformen für Hilfsverben

	können	dürfen	müssen	sollen
simple present	can, be able to	can, be allowed to, may	must, have/has to	should, ought to
***will*-future**	will be able to	will be allowed to	will have to	will be supposed to
present perfect	have/has been able to	have/has been allowed to	have/has had to	has been supposed to
simple past	could, was/were able to	could, was/were allowed to	had to	was supposed to
past perfect	had been able to	had been allowed to	had had to	had been supposed to

Verneinung und Frage mit *have to*

have to wird wie ein Vollverb verneint, auch Fragen werden wie bei Vollverben gebildet.

I don't have to go to school today.
Do you have to go to school today?

I didn't have to go to school today.
Did you have to go to school today?

I won't have to go to school tomorrow.
Will you have to go to school tomorrow?

5.1 Questions and negations

2

Here are some answers. What were the questions? Write them down.

Example:
Mr. Mathews: Of course you must do your homework.
Students: Must we do the homework?

Here are some answers Mr. Mathews gave to questions his new class asked him during the first lesson of the year.

1. Of course I can play football.

___

___

2. No, you may not eat during class.

___

___

3. Yes, you are allowed to chew gum during class tests.

___

___

4. No, you may not ask your parents for help when you don't know how to do your homework.

___

___

5. Yes, you may go to the bathroom.

___

___

5.2 Negative form

3

In the second lesson Mr. Mathews asked his students to write down rules for their dream school. Unfortunately, dreams are just dreams, and don't often have much to do with reality … Read the students' rules, and write down the real rules after them.

Example:
Students may sleep in late every day.
Students may not sleep in late every day.

1. Students are allowed to come to school whenever they want to.

   ____

   ____

2. Teachers have to give good marks for every class test.

   ____

   ____

3. Students may talk during class as much as they want.

   ____

   ____

4. Teachers have to cook lunch for the students every day.

   ____

   ____

5. Students are allowed to listen to music during the lessons.

   ____

   ____

5.3 Being polite

4

If you want to be polite you can use the following modals:

very polite may could can *not so polite*

Write the questions in English.

1. Du fragst den Direktor deiner Schule, ob du nach Hause gehen darfst.

2. Du fragst deine Nachbarin und beste Freundin, ob du ihren Stift leihen darfst.

3. Du fragst einen Schüler, der drei Jahre älter ist, ob er dir mit der Matheaufgabe helfen kann.

4. Du fragst einen Klassenkameraden, ob du seine Hausaufgaben abschreiben* kannst.

5. Du fragst deine Klassenlehrerin, ob du die Frage beantworten darfst.

*Hausaufgaben abschreiben – **to copy homework**

5.4 Expressing uncertainty

5

You can use the following modals to express how sure – or not – you are about something:

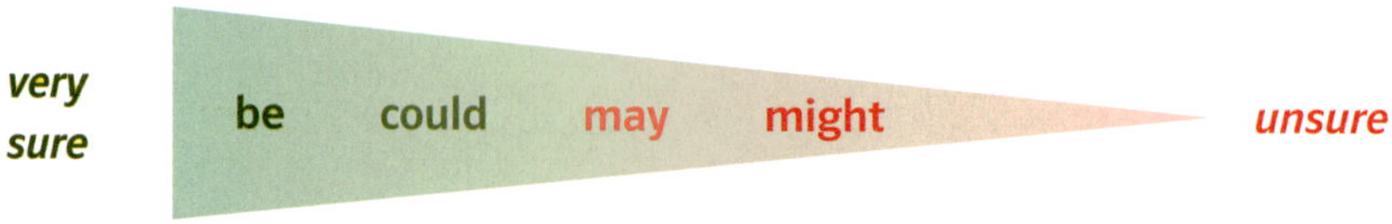

Fill in the gaps using the correct modal.

This may be an exercise book.

1. This ____________________ a playground.

2. This ____________________.

3. This ____________________.

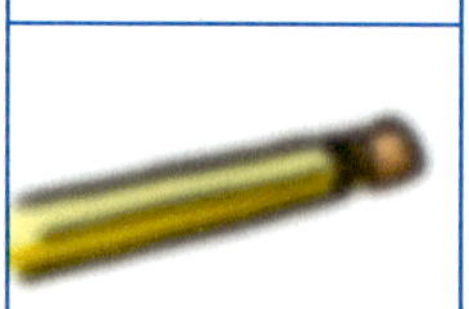

4. This ____________________.

5. This ____________________.

6. This ____________________.

5.5 Giving advice

6

If you want to give someone advice, you can use modals to express how important it is.

necessary **should** **must** **have to** *extremely necessary*

Fill in the gaps using the correct modal.

Father: You really should work harder for Spanish, Jim.

(Ein „D" in Amerika entspricht etwa einer „4" in Deutschland.)

1. *Mother:* You ________________ work harder for Spanish, Mary.

(Ein „F" in Amerika entspricht etwa einer „6" in Deutschland.)

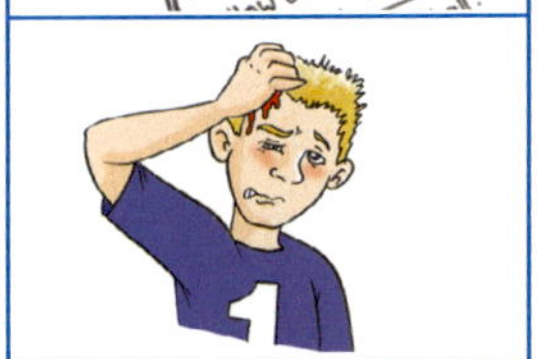

2. *Teacher:* I think you ________________ go home and see a doctor, Simon.

3. *Teacher (to himself):* I ________________ find a new job.

4. *Student:* Why doesn't anybody do something? Someone ________________ call a doctor!

5. *Neighbour:* I think you ________________ wake up, Stan.

5.6 Replacements

7

Rewrite the rules below in full sentences, using the modal given.

Example: Arrive on time. **(must)**

Students must arrive on time.

These are rules from an American High School.

1. Raise your hand before speaking. **(must)**
2. Listen to each other. **(should)**
3. Cooperate with your group. **(ought to)**
4. Leave other people's materials alone. **(ought to)**
5. Do not interrupt other students' learning. **(may not)**
6. Don't write or carve on your desk or other school property. **(may not)**
7. Treat computers with care. **(must)**
8. Absolutely no gum, candy or other food. **(to be allowed to eat)**
9. Be organized and prepared for class. **(ought to)**

1. Students ______________________________.
2. Students ______________________________.
3. Everyone ______________________________.
4. Everyone ______________________________
______________________________.
5. Class members ______________________________
______________________________.
6. Students ______________________________
______________________________.
7. Everybody ______________________________.
8. Absolutely no one ______________________________
______________________________.
9. Everyone ______________________________.

8

Now rewrite the sentences from exercise 7 in the tense given for each sentence, using a substitute form where necessary.

Examples:

simple past: *Students had to arrive on time.*

will-future: *Students will have to arrive on time.*

past perfect: *Students have had to arrive on time.*

1. *will*-future: ______________________________

____

2. simple past: ______________________________

____

3. past perfect: ______________________________

____

4. simple past: ______________________________

____

5. *will*-future: ______________________________

____

6. *will*-future: ______________________________

____

7. present perfect: ______________________________

____

8. *will*-future: ______________________________

____

9. past perfect: ______________________________

____

5.7 Summing it up

9 10

Fill in the gaps using the correct modal. The German verb in brackets will help you choose the modal verb. You can listen to the CD to check your answers.

A week later Mr. Mathews gave back a class test that had been very bad. He was upset that his class had got such bad marks, and he talked to them about the test:

Mr. Mathews: Good morning, class. I have corrected your class tests and I ______________________ **(konnte)** find a single good one. What went wrong? I ______________________ **(muss)** admit, I was quite surprised and at the same time very sad. We really ______________________ **(müssen)** talk about this. I ______________________ **(kann nicht)** believe that you didn't understand anything I have been trying to teach you. Maybe I ______________________ **(sollte)** look for a new job. But ______________________ **(darf)** I ask you a question before I do this? How many of you think they didn't practice enough for this test? What – all of you? Oh, so it wasn't all my fault. You really ______________________ **(müsst)** prepare better for the tests if you want to get good grades. ______________________ **(soll)** I talk to your parents about this? No? None of you want me to talk to your parents about this? OK, then we have to make a deal: you promise to work harder in this class, and I won't tell your parents about this disaster.

After class the students are talking to each other:

Alice: My parents will kill me if they find out about this test! But I'm so bad at Spanish. I think I ______________________________ **(brauche)** extra help.

Margaret: But then you ______________________________ **(solltest)** tell your parents about the test. If you don't tell them, they ______________________________ **(können nicht)** know that you're having problems learning Spanish.

Joe: Oh come on, I think the test was too difficult anyway. I think Mathews ______________________________ **(sollte)** make the tests easier. We are such a nice class.

Claire: Well, he ______________________________ **(wird vielleicht)** make the next test easier if we give him a little present.

Arthur: Oh, come on – you know he ______________________________ **(darf nicht)** do that. He would lose his job.

Alice: Hmm, sounds like I ______________________________ **(werde wohl)** be killed this afternoon. See you in heaven. Do they have Spanish tests there?

1

Cross out the odd one!

1.	may	to be allowed to	must	might
2.	must	might	have to	should
3.	ought to	may	could	might
4.	should	ought to	could	shall

points: 4 *one point for each correct answer*

2

What's the next sentence? Tick the correct answer!

I'm very late for class.	I must hurry.	☐
	I needn't hurry.	☐
You look tired.	Yes, I really need to sleep more.	☐
	Yes, I ought to get up earlier.	☐
She looks really unhappy.	Yes, she needs to work harder for school.	☐
	Yes, she might have done badly in another bad test.	☐
Pete is very bad in English. If he fails the test, he will have to leave school.	Pete needn't pass the test.	☐
	Pete must pass the test.	☐

points: 4 one *point for each question*

3 11

Fill in the gaps using the correct modal! You can listen to the CD to check your answers.

Alice is afraid of the next class test.

Joe: Hi Alice. I thought you were dead.

Alice: Well, my parents let me live. I ________________ **(musste)** to promise to get better in Spanish, though. ________________ **(kannst)** you *please* help me?

Joe: What do you want me to do?

Alice: You ________________ **(könntest)** sit next to me next time.

Joe: You really ________________ **(darfst nicht)** look at me like that.

I ________________ **(vielleicht)** fall in love with you and then

I ________________ **(vielleicht)** do stupid things.

Alice: Oh Joey, I'll be lost without you. I ________________ **(brauche)** your help or I'll be lost forever.

Joe: Maybe I ________________ **(kann)** just help you prepare for the next test.

Alice: But what if that doesn't help? Oh Joey, what ________________ **(soll)** I do?

Joe: First of all you ________________ **(musst)** relax. Spanish isn't the only thing in the world. You really ________________ **(solltest)** think of other things. For example the new movie at the cinema. You ________________ **(musst)** see it, it's great.

Alice: ________________ **(könntest)** you please be serious?

Joe: No, I ________________ **(kann nicht)**, I'm in love with a girl that ________________ **(kann nicht)** speak Spanish.

one point for each gap points: 15

0–11 points ☹	12–18 points 😐	19–23 points ☺
You've made quite a lot of mistakes – you should read this chapter again!	That was OK, but you can do better!	You did a really good job!

maximum number of points: 23

6 Reported speech

1 Check-up

Match what the people said with what Christopher and Erica tell Anna.

When Christopher and Erica went on a trip with their parents two years ago, they secretly recorded what people said at a youth hostel. Now they are playing this recording to their exchange student Anna, who has difficulty understanding the recording. So they have to repeat it for her.

1. I may come back very late tonight.
2. Can I have the keys to my room, please!
3. Have you ever travelled alone?
4. I like long bus rides.
5. My parents will take me to Hawaii next summer.
6. I spent last winter in Europe with my friends.
7. When does the next bus to New York leave?
8. I'm going to stay in the cheapest hotel in Manhattan.
9. Don't tell my girlfriend that I went out late.

a. *Christopher:* A little boy told someone that he liked long bus rides. ◯

b. *Erica:* An older traveller mentioned that he had spent the previous* winter in Europe with his friends. ◯

c. *Christopher:* A girl in a dress said that she might come back very late that night. ◯

d. *Erica:* A backpacker asked his friend when the next bus to New York left. ◯

e. *Christopher:* A young girl said her parents would take her to Hawaii the following summer. ◯

f. *Erica:* A drunk guy asked the receptionist to give him the keys to his room. ◯

g. *Christopher:* A good-looking teenager told his friend not to tell his girlfriend that he had gone out late. ◯

h. *Erica:* A girl with red hair asked someone whether she had ever travelled alone. ◯

i. *Christopher:* Another very dirty-looking guy said that he was going to stay in the cheapest hotel in Manhattan. ◯

***previous** – vorherig(e)

Die indirekte Rede

"I spent last winter in Europe with my friends."
He said (that) he had spent the previous winter in Europe with **his** friends.

Alles, was im zweiten Satz rot hervorgehoben ist, hat sich verändert:

1. Vor den Satz, den du wiederholst, stellst du ein einleitendes Verb (*he said*).
2. *that* verwendet man nur in Aussagen, es kann auch weggelassen werden.
3. Die Personalpronomina verändern sich, denn du gibst wieder, was jemand anderes gesagt hat, und **dessen/deren Freund** ist nicht **dein Freund** sondern **sein oder ihr** Freund.
4. Die Zeitform des Verbs (*tense*) ändert sich.
5. Orts- und Zeitangaben verändern sich, da sich die Perspektive verändert. Was für denjenigen, der gerade spricht, nahe ist (*here, last winter*), ist für den, der erzählt, was gesagt worden ist, weit weg (*there, the previous winter*).

Verben zur Einleitung der indirekten Rede *(reporting verbs)*

Aussagen *(positive statements)*		**Fragen** *(questions)*	**Befehle / Bitten** *(orders / requests)*
say	explain	ask someone	ask someone
mention	think	want to know	tell someone
believe	write	wonder	warn someone
tell s.o.	answer		

Veränderung der Personalpronomen

direct speech	**reported speech**
I	he / she / (it)
you	I (Subjekt) / me (Objekt)
he / she / it	unverändert
we	they
you	we (Subjekt) / us (Objekt)
they	we

Zeitformen in indirekter Rede

direct speech	reported speech
present "I **like** long bus rides."	**past** He said that he **liked** long bus rides.
past "I **spent** last winter in Europe."	**past perfect** He mentioned that he **had spent** the previous winter in Europe.
present perfect "**Have** you ever **travelled** alone?"	**past perfect** He wondered if I **had** ever **travelled** alone.
***will*-future** "My parents **will take** me on a trip to Hawaii."	**would + infinitive** He told us that his parents **would take** him on a trip to Hawaii.
***going to*-future** "I'**m going to stay** in the cheapest hotel in Manhattan."	**was/were + going to + infinitive** She said that he **was going to stay** in the cheapest hotel in Manhattan.
may "I **may** come back very late tonight."	**might** Someone said that he **might** be very late that night.
can "**Can** I have the keys to my room, please!"	**could** Someone asked me if I **could** give him the keys to his room.

Verben im *past pefect* sowie *should, could, would, might, must* und *needn't* bleiben unverändert.

Ortsangaben

direct speech	reported speech
here	there

Zeitangaben

direct speech	reported speech
now	then, at that time
today	that day, on that day
yesterday	the day before / the previous day
tomorrow	the following/next day
next year	the following year
two years ago	two years earlier

Fragen in der indirekten Rede

Die Satzstellung von Fragen in der indirekten Rede ist die gleiche wie in Aussagesätzen: Subjekt – Prädikat – Objekt (SPO).

Entscheidungsfragen *(yes/no questions)*

"Have you ever travelled alone?"	He wanted to know **if / whether** I had ever travelled alone.

Die Frage in der indirekten Rede wird mit *if* oder *whether* (deutsch „ob“) eingeleitet.

Fragen mit Fragewort

"When does the next bus to New York leave?"	He asked **when** the next bus to New York left.

Das Fragewort wird beibehalten.

Befehle und Bitten

"Can I have the keys to my room, please!" "Don't tell my girlfriend that I went out late."	He **asked me to give** him the keys to his room. "He told his friend **not to tell** his girlfriend that he had gone out late."

Normalerweise bilden wir Bitten und Befehle mit *ask someone* oder *tell someone* und einer Infinitivkonstruktion.

Gefühlsausdrücke oder Höflichkeitsfloskeln wie *please, oh* etc. kann man in der Regel weglassen.

6.1 Positive and negative statements in reported speech

2 12

What did Christopher and Erica tell Anna about what they had heard? You can listen to the CD to check your answers.

At school, Christopher and Erica told their friends about their trip and they were given a lot of tips about where they should go. Anna wasn't at school with them, so Erica wrote everything down. At home, Christopher and Erica tell Anna what their friends had said:

Erik: It's a long way to travel.
Pete: Las Vegas is great.
Kyle: New Orleans is not a good place to go because it's too far south.
Connie: Mesa Verde is very interesting because you can see the Indian cave-dwellings.
Suzanne: Florida is beautiful, and you can go swimming there and see the alligators in Everglades National Park.
Marianne: Don't go to Kansas – it's boring.
Joey: The Great Lakes are fun.

1 cave-dwellings – Höhlenbehausungen

Christopher: Well, Erik explained that ______________________________

____,

but Pete said that ______________________________

____.

Erica: That's right, but Kyle told us ______________________________

______________________________ because it

______________________________. Yes,

hmmm, and Connie, oh yes, she thought ______________________________

______________________________ because

______________________________.

Christopher: You know, I think Suzanne is not very good at geography.

She told me that ______________________________

______________________________ because

____

______________________________.

Doesn't she know where Florida is?

Erica: Well, let's forget about this. Marianne told us ______________________________

______________________________ because

______________________________.

I think that's good to know.

Christopher: You're right. And Joey said ______________________________

______________________________.

Maybe we can go swimming there.

Anna: So where will we go? I'll go to a travel agency and find out more tomorrow.

6.2 Introductory verbs

3

Cross out the introductory verb(s) that can't be used in the following sentences. Sometimes all of the verbs are correct.

Of course, Anna told her family about the trip. She also wrote a letter to her grandmother. Here's what her parents and her grandmother wrote back.

Anna's mother **told / thought / asked** that it was a great idea to travel through America, but she also **mentioned / told / said** them to be very careful.
Anna's father was very excited and **explained / said / warned** that he had done a trip like that 30 years before.
However, he also **asked / told / explained** them to be careful, especially in the Alaskan wilderness.
Anna laughed and **explained / said / wrote** that they weren't planning on going to Alaska, so he could relax.
Her father **thought / believed / asked** that that was a good idea. He **wanted to know / wondered / thought** where they were planning on going instead.
Anna **said / answered / mentioned** that they hadn't made any plans.
Her father was very excited and he **told / said / wrote** her to visit a hundred wonderful places.
Half an hour later, Anna put down the phone and was very confused about her trip.
Then she wrote to her grandmother. She answered quickly, and in her letter she **asked / told / said** Anna that she was too young for such a trip and that she should rather stay at home.
She also **said / mentioned / explained** that America was too far away.
She **told / mentioned / asked** her to come home as fast as possible.
She also **believed / wrote / told** that America was full of gangsters and was a really dangerous place.
In the end she **warned / told / asked** Anna not to leave the house until her father could come and bring her back home.
When she showed this letter to Christopher and Erica they laughed. They **said / asked / thought** that grandparents were the same all over the world.

6.3 Questions in reported speech

4 13

Write down what the travel agent asked. Use the following reporting verbs: **ask**, **want to know**, **wonder**. You can listen to the CD to check your answers.

When Anna went to the travel agency the next day, she was asked a lot of questions. When she came home she told her friends what the lady had asked.

1. *Are you old enough to travel alone?*
2. *Do your parents know about your plans?*
3. *How much time do you have for your trip?*
4. *When do you want to leave?*
5. *How much money do you want to spend?*
6. *Will you go by train or by bus?*
7. *Do you want to visit National Parks or cities?*

Erica: What did you find out, Anna?

Anna: Not much really. The lady just asked a lot of questions and when I couldn't answer some of them, she told me to go home, find out, and then come back.

Christopher: Alright. What did she ask?

Anna: First, she asked if we were old enough to travel alone.

When I said "yes", she ____

____.

I replied that it had even been our parents' idea. That surprised her, but she went on and ____

____.

I told her that we had all summer. I think she was quite impressed but then she asked all the questions we hadn't talked about yet. She ______________

____,

then she ____

____

____.

When I told her that we didn't know, she sighed but went on and __________

____

____

and ____

____.

Again I had to tell her that we didn't know. Then she became a little unfriendly and told me to go home and talk to you about these questions, and not to come back before we had answers and knew what we wanted.

6.4 Commands and requests in reported speech

5 14

What does Erica remember about the things Christopher and Anna asked her to check on the internet? Use the following reporting verbs:
ask someone to do sth, **tell so to do sth**, **want sb to do sth**.
You can listen to the CD to check your answers.

Because Anna hadn't found out much, Erica decided to check the internet for information. Anna and Christopher had a lot of ideas about what to look for.

Christopher:
1. Please find out what a Greyhound ticket from here to New York costs.
2. Make sure to check if we can get off as often as we want to.
3. Please see if you can find out more about Mesa Verde.
4. See what there is on Chicago.
5. Oh, and hurry up, I want to check my e-mail.

Anna:
1. Please check where we can go by train.
2. Oh yes, and find out more about Kansas.
3. Check on chat-rooms to find out more about travelling in the US.
4. Oh, and write an e-mail to the lady at the travel agency and tell her that she was very unfriendly, and that we won't come back.

Erica: OK, let's start:

1. Christopher asked me ______________________________

   ____

   ______________________________.

2. He also ______________________________

   ____

   ______________________________.

3. Then ____
____
____.

4. He also ____
____
____.

5. Finally, ____
____
____.

Idiot!

Anna also had some interesting ideas. Let's see:

1. First she wanted me ____
____
____.

2. Then she ____
____
____.

Why is she interested in Kansas? It's so boring there. Anyway:

3. She also ____
____
____.

That was a good idea.

4. Finally, she ____
____
____.

Alright, that's it then.

6.5 Expressions of place and time and pronouns in reported speech

6 15

Read the comments from the homepage. Then fill in the gaps in Erica's report, using the correct expressions of place and time and the correct pronouns. You can listen to the CD to check your answers.

Erica tells Anna and Christopher what she learned from a homepage on travelling in the US.

Jason (2004)	You should definitely travel through Kansas, I have lived here all my life and I think it's great!
Anne (2005)	Don't go to Chicago: I hate it here. I moved here a year ago. All you will see here are cars, cars, cars and cars.
Allison (2007)	Mesa Verde is the greatest place of all. We arrived here yesterday and I hope we will stay until Tuesday. That's when there will be a special guided tour of the Native American sites.
Joey (2005)	My sister came back from her trip three days ago, and she was very excited about the Great Lakes. I think she is crazy because I was there last winter and it was freezing cold.

Erica:

Alright, here's what I found out: A guy called Jason wrote that __________ should definitely travel through Kansas. He said that __________ had lived __________ all __________ life and __________ thought it was great! Unfortunately he didn't tell us what was great. Well, then there was a girl called Anne. She warned us not to go to Chicago. She said that __________ hated it __________ and that __________ had moved __________ __________. She explained that all __________ would see __________ would be cars.

Then there was Allison. She was in Mesa Verde, and wrote that it was the greatest place of all. __________ had arrived __________ __________ and __________ hoped that __________ would stay until __________. That was when there would be a special guided tour of the Native American sites. That sounds good. And finally there was a note by a guy called Joey. He said that __________ sister had come back from her trip __________ and that she had been very excited about the Great Lakes. __________ thinks she was crazy because __________ had been there __________ __________ and it had been freezing cold.

So what do you think?

6.6 Summing it up

7 16

Rewrite the following statements in reported speech. You can listen to the CD to check your answers.

Five years after the trip, Anna visits Christopher and Erica again in California. They talk about their trip and look at pictures of the crazy people they had met. Then they try to remember what these people had said.

1. I have lost everything. Can you please give me some money?

2. My parents forgot me here. Can I come with you?

3. I will stay and live here. In three years you will all understand why.

4. Sure, I can give you a ride, ladies – but I don't take guys.

5. Have you thought about your lives? Someone might ask you soon.

6. If you kiss here, you will find everlasting love.

1. *Erica:* Do you remember the guy in Vegas?

   Anna: Yes, – he told us ______________________________

   and ______________________________.

2. *Christopher:* Oh, yes. That was the girl in Death Valley. She ______________

   ____

   and ______________________________.

3. *Erica:* Great. I loved the hippie woman. What did she say?

   Anna: She ______________________________

   ____

   and ______________________________

   ______________________________.

4. *Christopher:* Wow! That was the "super cool" idiot with his fancy car.

   Erica: Yes, he ______________________________

   ____

   but he also ______________________________

   ______________________________.

5. *Anna:* Yes, that was interesting. That was the priest in Colorado.

   He ______________________________

   ____

   and ______________________________.

   That was a little scary.

6. *Anna:* Oh, how romantic. Do you remember the couple on the Empire State Building?

   Christopher: Yes, how stupid. They ______________________________

   ____

   if ______________________________.

   Anna: Well, I'm glad I didn't try and kiss **you** there.

1

Find and correct the mistakes in the reported speech – some words may be missing, some may be wrong.

A boy tells his friends about a fight he had with his father two days earlier.

Father: Where are the pictures of my trip through America?
Son: I haven't seen them.
Father: Don't be stupid. I'm sure you had them yesterday.
Son: I'm really not interested in your pictures.
Father: I always keep them in my cupboard, but they aren't here now.
Mother: Look, Henry – why don't you take the ones right in front of you and leave your son alone?
Father: Hmm, that might be a good idea. Thank you, darling.

1. Yesterday my father told me where the pictures of his trip through America were.

   ____

2. I answered that I will not see them.

   ____

3. Then he told me not to be stupid and added that he was sure he had had them the day after.

   ____

4. I told that I really wasn't interested in his pictures.

   ____

5. Then dad said that he always kept them in her cupboard, but they weren't there.

   ____

6. Luckily, my mother came and wondered him why he didn't take the ones right in front of him and me alone.

   ____

7. My dad warned that that might be a good idea and thanked my mother.

   ____

points: 8 *one point for every mistake*

2

Put the following opinions about travelling into reported speech.

1. Travelling by train is dangerous because trains are too fast.

   A man in 1875 ______________________________

   ______________________________.

2. I'm afraid of travelling by plane. My cousin died in a plane crash five years ago.

   Last year a friend of mine ______________________________

   ____

   ______________________________.

3. My mother went to America by ship last year and she loved it.

   One of my classmates ______________________________

   ______________________________.

4. I'm going to fly to the moon as soon as possible because I hate life here.

   My pen friend from Australia ______________________________

   ____

   ______________________________.

5. Do you know how bad it is for the environment that everybody is flying around the world all the time?

   My brother ______________________________

   ____

   ______________________________.

two points for every sentence

points: ___ / 10

0–8 points ☹	9–13 points 😐	14–18 points ☺
You've made quite a lot of mistakes – you should read this chapter again!	That was OK, but you can do better!	You did a really good job!

maximum number of points: 18

Was ich bereits kann ...

Kreuze an, was für dich zutrifft.

	Kein Problem	Hier mache ich noch Fehler	Muss ich unbedingt noch üben
1 The past perfect simple and progressive			
1. Ich kann das *past perfect simple* bilden.			
2. Ich kann das *past perfect progressive* bilden.			
3. Ich weiß, wann man das *past perfect simple* und wann das *past perfect progressive* verwendet.			
2 Conditional sentences			
4. Ich kann erkennen, ob ein *conditional sentence* zum Typ I, II oder III gehört.			
5. Ich kann *conditional sentences type I* bilden.			
6. Ich kann *conditional sentences type II* bilden.			
7. Ich kann *conditional sentences type III* bilden.			
8. Ich kann aufgrund der Wahrscheinlichkeit einer Bedingung entscheiden, welchen Typ von *conditional sentence* ich anwenden muss.			
3 Relative clauses			
9. Ich erkenne, ob ein Relativsatz bestimmend *(defining)* oder ergänzend *(non-defining)* ist.			
10. Ich erkenne, ob ich einen Relativsatz verkürzen kann oder nicht.			

	Kein Problem	Hier mache ich noch Fehler	Muss ich unbedingt noch üben
11. Ich kenne die wichtigsten Unterschiede zwischen bestimmenden und ergänzenden Realtivsätzen.			
12. Ich kann Relativsätze mit satzbezüglichem *which* bilden.			

4 Talking about the future

13. Ich kenne die vier verschiedenen Zeitformen, die das Englische für die Zukunft hat.			
14. Ich kann all diese Zeitformen bilden.			
15. Ich kann entscheiden, wann ich welche Form benötige.			

5 Modal auxiliaries and their replacements

16. Ich weiß, was ein modales Hilfsverb ist.			
17. Ich kann modale Hilfsverben in englischen Sätzen korrekt verwenden.			
18. Ich kenne wichtige modale Hilfsverben und ihre Ersatzformen.			

6 Reported speech

19. Ich kenne die wichtigsten Unterschiede zwischen direkter und indirekter Rede.			
20. Ich kenne verschiedene *reporting verbs* zur Einleitung der indirekten Rede.			
21. Ich kann direkte Rede in indirekte Rede umformen.			

Vocabulary

HEY, WHAT ARE YOU DOING THERE?
I'M PAINTING A PAINTING.
I'M BUILDING A BUILDING.
FUNNY, DO YOU HEAR AN ECHO?
NO, JUST POOR VOCABULARY.

7 American and British English

1 Check-up

Which of these sentences are American (AE) and which are British English (BE)? If you answer correctly, the letters will spell out an important difference between AE and BE!

Would you like to see my apartment?	S	O
Would you like to see my flat?	A	P
That's my favorite color.	E	U
That's my favourite colour.	C	L
Can I use your bathroom, please?	L	I
Can I use your toilet please?	L	I
Would you like to go to the theatre with me tonight?	P	N
Would you like to go to the theater with me tonight?	G	A

An important difference between American English and British English is ____________________________.

Amerikanisches und britisches Englisch

Englisch wird fast überall auf der Welt gesprochen – und überall ein bisschen anders. Bis jetzt hast du im Englischunterricht hauptsächlich *British English* (BE) gelernt. In diesem Jahr erfährst du, wie in Amerika gesprochen und geschrieben wird (AE).
Die Unterschiede sind zwar nicht allzu groß, dennoch können leicht Missverständnisse entstehen. Hier lernst du die wichtigen Unterscheidungsmerkmale kennen.

Schreibung

Die Schreibweise ist für das Verständnis des Inhalts nicht so wichtig. Du kannst in deinem Computer einstellen, ob BE oder AE korrigiert wird.

BE	AE	BE	AE	BE	AE
-our	**-or**	**-gramme**	**-gram**	**-re**	**-er**
colour favourite neighbour harbour behaviour	color favorite neighbor harbor behavior	programme	program	theatre metre centre	theater meter center

Aussprache 17–19

Die Beispiele für die unterschiedliche Aussprache von BE und AE findest du auch auf der CD.

17	possible, hot, problem	half, after	student, Tuesday
BE	[ɒ]	[ɑː]	[juː]
AE	[ɔ]	[æː]	[uː]

Außerdem sprechen die Amerikaner das „r" aus, während es bei den Briten in der Regel entfällt:

understand, other, word **18**

Schließlich klingt das amerikanische „t" oft wie ein „d"

water, better, butter **19**

Wortschatz

Das größte Problem entsteht, wenn verschiedene Wörter für ein und dieselbe Sache verwendet werden. Wir beschränken uns in diesem Kapitel auf die Wortfelder Haus, Schule und Stadt.

Wortfeld Haus

BE	AE	Deutsch
flat	apartment	Wohnung
back garden	back yard	Garten (hinter dem Haus)
lift	elevator	Aufzug
veranda	porch	Terasse
pavement	sidewalk	Gehweg
toilet	restroom / bathroom	WC
postman	mailman	Postbote
ground floor	first floor	Erdgeschoss

Wortfeld Schule

BE	AE	Deutsch
class / form	grade	Klassen(stufe)
mark	grade	Note
head teacher / headmaster / headmistress	principal	Rektor/-in
pupil	student	Schüler/-in
caretaker	janitor	Hausmeister/-in
holidays	vacation	Ferien
primary school	elementary school	Grundschule
comprehensive school	high school	weiterführende Schule
exercise book	notebook	Heft
timetable	schedule	Stundenplan

Wortfeld Stadt

BE	AE	Deutsch
film	movie	Spielfilm
at the cinema	at the movies	im Kino
underground	subway	U-Bahn
city centre	downtown	Stadtzentrum
shop	store	Geschäft
to stand in a queue	to stand in line	Schlange stehen
car park	parking lot	Parkplatz
shopping centre	shopping mall	Einkaufszentrum

7.1 Spelling

2

Change the underlined words into American English.

Mark is from Manchester. He is spending half a year at his uncle's house in Phoenix (Arizona). He goes to school there, and when he gets back his first homework he sees that his English teacher has marked a lot of mistakes – he was expected to write American English. Take a red pen and write the American English words over the "mistakes".

favorite

My ~~favourite~~ place in the world

I once saw a programme on television that showed a little island somewhere far away. I loved it. It was about 200 metres long and 100 metres wide. The water around it was incredible, too. The colours just made me go crazy. Green, turquoise, blue … In the centre of the island stood a coconut tree about as tall as a house. They taste so much better than the ones you buy in the supermarket. In fact their flavour is totally different. I think I would like to spend a holiday there without neighbours …

7.2 Pronounciation

3 20–23

Listen to the sentences on the CD, and decide whether they are BE or AE.

After four weeks Mark goes to a meeting of the British exchange students in Arizona. Their American hosts are there, too. Here is what the people said.

Sentence no.	1	2	3	4	5	6	7	8
	☐	☐	☐	☐	☐	☐	☐	☐
	☐	☐	☐	☐	☐	☐	☐	☐

7.3 Words

4

Put the letters on the left into the correct order to find the BE words, then find the AE synonym in the grid.

After his experience with the homework, Marc decides to teach his American classmates some of the differences between AE and BE. Here's what he came up with:

	BE	AE
filt		
sydiloha		
mifl		
lupip		
tetoil		
gorunundder		
kram		
mostpan		
psoh		
recerakat		

e	m	a	t	g	r	a	d	e	p	k
r	o	v	v	a	c	a	t	i	o	n
h	v	g	h	a	h	u	k	m	n	v
s	i	u	s	m	a	i	l	m	a	n
u	e	j	t	s	o	u	z	g	l	f
b	d	g	o	n	n	h	o	l	i	s
w	u	k	r	u	e	b	h	u	f	a
a	e	l	e	v	a	t	o	r	t	t
y	l	o	b	a	t	h	r	o	o	m
e	j	a	n	i	t	o	r	d	h	k
l	d	c	o	p	d	k	i	z	f	d
s	t	u	d	e	n	t	s	h	u	t

5

Are the underlined words British or American English? If they are AE then change them into BE.

After a few weeks Marc is so confused by the different kinds of English that he mixes the two up all the time. He wrote a letter home to his parents – and got them all mixed up.

Hello Mum and Dad,

Yesterday I was ~~downtown~~ in the city centre with some pupils from my class. We were at the movies. It was great, although we had to stand in line for a long time for the tickets. The film was amazing (it was a horror movie). It was about a postman who was attacked by a dog in the back yard of a house. The dog had jumped from a window on the ground floor onto the porch and then almost killed the mailman. After he had left hospital he decided to kill the dog, and went to the shopping mall to buy a gun. I don't think you'll want to hear the rest of the story, because it gets really scary. At school nothing really important happened, only that I lost my exercise book. So now I will get a bad grade for that class. I asked the caretaker if he had found it, but he hadn't. The headmaster of my cousin Sarah's elementary school has decided that their summer vacation will be a week longer. I'm jealous. If I had a week more of summer vacation I would go to Las Vegas and win a lot of money for you.

Bye

Marc

1 24

Decide whether the sentence was spoken in AE or in BE.

Sentence no.	1	2	3	4	5	6
BE	☐	☐	☐	☐	☐	☐
AE	☐	☐	☐	☐	☐	☐

one point for every correct answer — *points:* 6

2

Rewrite the following text in British English.

A month later, Marc was so used to living in America that his letter home was all in AE … He even calls his Mum "Mom" now!

Dear Mom and Dad,

Last week a student from my school gave a party. He lives downtown right next to the theater. As a present I bought him the latest CD by his favorite hip-hop band. I had bought it at the shopping mall near school. The party was great. We were allowed to use the porch and the back yard, and they let us dance until early in the morning. The neighbors didn't care at all, which was also great. In the center of the lawn they had a little bar with soft drinks* so we could take one any time we wanted. It was just great. Sometimes it's really nice to be in a house and not a small apartment like we have back home in Manchester. Our vacations start next week and then my time here will almost be over. I have enjoyed it a lot. Thank you very much for giving me the chance to live here for a while. I have learned so many new things. I'm only afraid of my first English test back home. I'm sure I will get a bad grade because of all my American English. Well, life is not always fair, is it?

Love
Marc

*__soft drink__ – alkoholfreies Getränk

one point for each correct change — *points:* 12

0–8 points ☹	9–13 points 😐	14–18 points ☺
You've made quite a lot of mistakes – you should read this chapter again!	That was OK, but you can do better!	You did a really good job!

maximum number of points: 18

8 Building words

1 Check-up

a) Which noun goes with the verb in the middle?

to invite: invitement, inviting, invitation

to discuss: discussion, discussment, discuss

to move: movement, movation, moving

to surprise: surprise, surprising, surprisation

b) Which is the opposite of the word on the left?

certain	↔	uncertain	incertain	discertain
possible	↔	impossible	unpossible	inpossible
active	↔	disactive	imactive	inactive
to lock	↔	to dislock	to inlock	to unlock

Wortbildung

Die Kenntnis einiger Grundregeln der Wortbildung hilft dir dabei, deinen Wortschatz zu erweitern.
Durch das Anhängen von Nachsilben (Suffixen) kann z. B. aus einem Verb ein Substantiv werden. Leider gibt es keine Regel, welches Suffix an welche Art von Verb gehängt wird.

Substantive bilden

Das Suffix *-ion*

to discuss	→	discussion
to collect	→	collection

Das Suffix *-ation*

to invite	→	invitation
to explain	→	explanation
to organize	→	organization

Das Suffix *-ment*

to move	→	movement
to disappoint	→	disappointment
to treat	→	treatment

Das Suffix *-ing*

to feel	→	feeling
to mean	→	meaning
to paint	→	painting

Das Suffix *-er/-or*

Das Suffix *-er* oder *-or* drückt oft eine Person aus, die etwas macht.

to swim	→	swimmer
to work	→	worker
to instruct	→	instructor

Substantiv und Verb mit gleicher Form

to number	→	number
to list	→	list
to surprise	→	surprise

Adjektive bilden

Durch Voranstellen einer Vorsilbe (Präfix) kann man die Bedeutung eines Adjektivs verändern.

Präfixe *un-, in-, im-, ir-*
Präfixe verkehren oft die Bedeutung des Adjektivs in das Gegenteil, z. B. *un-, in-, im-, ir-*.

popular	→	unpopular
able	→	unable
correct	→	incorrect
expensive	→	inexpensive
regular	→	irregular
possible	→	impossible

Adjektive aus Substantiven: das Suffix *-less*
Durch das Suffix *-less* kann man aus Substantiven Adjektive machen. Die Bedeutung wird dadurch in das Gegenteil verkehrt:
hope (Hoffnung) – *hopeless* – es gibt keine Hoffnung.

end	→	endless
hope	→	hopeless
sleep	→	sleepless

Adjektive aus Substantiven: das Suffix *-ful*
Durch das Suffix *-ful* kann man aus Substantiven Adjektive machen. Das Adjektiv verstärkt dann die Bedeutung des Substantivs:
thanks (Dank) – *thankful* (dankbar).

thanks	→	thankful
use	→	useful
beauty	→	beautiful

8.1 Nouns

2

Build a noun! Which of the two suffixes works better? Or does the word not take a suffix (—)?

to invite		
-ing	-ation	

to butter		
-ment	—	

to combine		
-ation	-or	

to run		
-or	-er	

to nail		
—	-ing	

to travel		
-ment	-er	

to end		
—	-ing	

8.2 Adjectives

3

Use prefixes to build the opposites of the words given.

employed		
im-	un-	

lucky		
un-	ir-	

correct		
in-	im-	

perfect		
un-	im-	

natural		
ir-	un-	

interesting		
un-	im-	

exact		
un-	in-	

active		
ir-	in-	

4

Add *-less* or *-ful* to form an adjective.

joy		head	
sense		life	
wonder		truth	

8.3 Summing it up

5

The first sentences contain underlined words – use the correct verb or noun forms of these words to fill in the gaps in the second sentences.

Is cow tipping an exciting hobby?

Example:
Last week Alan **invited** me to come to his house.
Last week I got an invitation from Alan to come to his house.

1. I was **surprised** when he **suggested** that we should go cow tipping.

   To my ________________ his ____________________ was that we should go cow tipping.

2. He said that cow tipping **combined** fun and exercise.

   He said that cow tipping was a _________________ of fun and exercise.

3. I then asked him **to explain** to me what exactly cow tipping was.

   I then asked him for an ______________________ of what cow tipping exactly was.

4. He was very **excited** when he told me that the idea of cow tipping was to run against cows while they were sleeping, so that they fell over. Of course that only works because cows stand when they sleep.

   Full of ____________________ he told me that the idea of cow tipping was to run against cows while they were sleeping, so that they fell over.

5. He was very **surprised** and **disappointed** when I said that this was not a good way to **treat** animals, and that I thought that we should **protect** them from people who do such terrible things.

   To his great ________________ and __________________________,
   I said that this was not a good __________________ of animals and that I thought that they needed ____________________ from the kind of people who do such stupid things.

6

Fill in the gaps using the opposites of the adjectives in the box.

probable	responsible	
possible	correct	able
conscious	believable	

Cow tipping is a myth*

I am a cattle farmer, and I have to tell you that cow tipping is ______________________. It is a popular myth that city people invented to make fun of people who live in the country. It is ______________________ that cows sleep standing up. They lie down to sleep. But even if they were standing, you would be ______________________ to sneak up on them, because they would hear and smell you from far away. It is also highly ______________________ that you would be able to tip a cow – they are *very* heavy. As a matter of fact it would be extremely funny to see one of these town people running against a cow, bouncing off, and then being kicked in the head. I'm not sure if I would carry his ______________________ body from the field. All in all I think it is ______________________ of people to invent stupid stories like this, but it is even more ______________________ that people believe them.

* **myth** – Mythos; Märchen

7

Fill in the gaps using the words from the box. The German words in brackets will help you choose the correct form of the word.

make a noun		
to laugh	to excite	to hate
to act	to believe	to kill
	to punish	

make an adjective	
forgivable	expensive
responsible	to respect

Opinions on cow tipping

1. I think cow tipping is great. It's an ______________________ **(billig)** way to spend your free time and it's a lot of fun. *(Joey, 18; Illinois)*
2. Cow tipping is a crime and it is ______________________ **(unverzeihlich)**. *(Bill, 35; New York)*
3. What's the big ______________________ **(Aufregung)** about cow tipping? Just accept that it's a joke that somebody made up. It's just a big ______________________ **(Witz)**. *(Alice, New Jersey; 16)*
4. I think cow tipping is the most ______________________ **(unverantwortungsvoll)** thing anyone can do. I can't describe the ______________________ **(Hass)** I feel for the terrible people who perform ______________________ **(Handlungen)** like this. *(an animal rights supporter from Nevada)*
5. The people in my hometown in Oklahoma share the ______________________ **(Glaube)** that cows are noble animals, and we should be more ______________________ **(respektvoll)** towards them. Because of that we call all cow tippers "______________________ **(Mörder)** of the cows' honor". We believe that the ______________________ **(Strafe)** cannot be severe* enough. *(Carl, 25; President of the "Honor the Cows' Honor Society", Iowa)*

* **severe** – streng

1

Cross out the words that don't exist.

to mean	meanment	meaning
to number	number	numbertion
to swim	swimmor	swimmer
to use	useless	usefull
expensive	expenseful	inexpensive
possible	impossible	inpossible
end	endles	ending

points: *one point for each word*

2

Read the text and fill in the gaps using the words from the table.
Which are the correct prefixes and suffixes?

prefix	word	suffix
un- im-	lucky beauty end speech discuss sense able use explain treat possible	-ful -less -ion -tion -ment

Claire has written an article about cow tipping for the school newspaper.

How stupid can people be?

Have you ever heard about cow tipping? You haven't. Let me tell you: you're lucky. I'm one of the ____________________ people who have.

I spent my vacations in the ____________________ state of Oklahoma, with its ______________________ prairies and all these nice people. But then one day someone asked me what I thought of cow-tipping. After he had explained it to me, I was ______________________ at first. Then I told him that this was the sickest thing I had ever heard of. We ended up having a long ______________________ about this totally ______________________ way of spending one's free time. He told me I couldn't talk about it if I hadn't tried doing it at least once. He was obviously ______________________ to understand how someone could care for something as "______________________" as a cow. All my ______________________ about animal rights and the correct ______________________ of other living beings didn't seem to affect him at all. Finally I just left the room and decided never to talk to this ______________________ person again. So if you ask me about the worst thing that happened to me during my vacation: this was it.

Claire

one point for every gap — points: 11

0 – 5 points ☹	6 – 10 points 😐	11 – 18 points ☺
You've made quite a lot of mistakes – you should read this chapter again!	That was OK, but you can do better!	You did a really good job!

maximum number of points: 18

Was ich bereits kann ...

Kreuze an, was für dich zutrifft.

	Kein Problem	Hier mache ich noch Fehler	Muss ich unbedingt noch üben
7 American and British English			
1. Ich kenne drei Unterschiede in der Schreibung zwischen britischem und amerikanischem Englisch.			
2. Ich kenne einige Unterschiede in der Aussprache zwischen britischem und amerikanischem Englisch.			
3. Ich kenne einige Unterschiede im Vokabular zwischen britischem und amerikanischem Englisch.			
8 Building words			
4. Ich kenne mindestens vier Suffixe, die mir helfen Substantive zu bilden.			
5. Ich kann die Bedeutung von Adjektiven mit Hilfe von Präfixen in ihr Gegenteil verwandeln.			

Understanding English

9 Reading comprehension

1 Check-up

Tick the correct answer.

In Seattle

A This sign …

- ☐ a. … tells you that you can see flying fish in an aquarium here.
- ☐ b. … warns you to be careful because this is an area where you may get hit by flying fish.
- ☐ c. … asks you to buy flying fish at a low price.

B This sign …

- ☐ a. … explains that you can see how ripe a tomato is by its color.
- ☐ b. … tells you that only soft tomatoes are ripe.
- ☐ c. … offers soft tomatoes at a low price.

Einen geschriebenen Text verstehen

Die Hauptaussage des Textes verstehen *(reading for gist)*

Wie beim Hören eines Textes wirst du auch beim Lesen oft einige Wörter nicht auf Anhieb verstehen. Anders als beim Hören hast du beim Lesen aber den Vorteil, dass du den Text mehrfach lesen kannst. Deshalb ist es – gerade in der Fremdsprache – sinnvoll, den Text zunächst einmal auf seine Hauptaussage hin zu lesen und sich nicht um Details zu kümmern. Beim ersten Lesen solltest du dich also besonders auf einige wenige wichtige Teile des Textes konzentrieren:

1. Überschriften
2. Anfang und Ende der jeweiligen Absätze (oder des Textes)
3. Fettgedrucktes oder Hervorgehobenes
4. Bilder

Einzelheiten verstehen *(reading for detail)*

Es passiert immer wieder, dass du Wörter in einem Text nicht verstehst. In der Regel kannst du sie aber erschließen. Folgende Techniken und Strategien helfen dir dabei:

1. Oft ähnelt das englische Wort einem deutschen – dann ist es besonders einfach (*fish* – Fisch).
2. Oft kennst du ein Wort derselben Wortfamilie (*exciting* (Adj.) – *excitement* (Subst.)).
3. Bei zusammengesetzten Wörtern kennst du möglicherweise eines oder gar beide Teile des Wortes (*house* + *wife* – *housewife*).
4. Vielleicht kennst du ein ähnliches Wort in einer anderen Sprache (engl.: *pardon me* – franz.: *pardonnez-moi*).
5. Schließlich wird es dir oft gelingen, die Bedeutung eines Wortes aus dem Zusammenhang zu erschließen. (Wenn dein Nachbar beim Schüleraustausch in Amerika mit dem Bleistift in der Hand sagt: *„Oh, I've made a mistake. Can I borrow your eraser?"* wirst du ihm mit Sicherheit deinen Radiergummi geben und nicht deinen Tintenkiller.)
6. Manchmal musst du im Wörterbuch nachschlagen oder jemanden fragen.
7. Schließlich musst du beim Erschließen von Wörtern immer auf der Hut sein: Der Satz muss einen Sinn ergeben! Wenn du zum Beispiel sagst: *„You've got a pickle on your nose"*, teilst du mit, dass auf der Nase eine Gewürzgurke ist. Diese etwas gemeinen Wörter heißen ***false friends***.

9.1 Reading for gist

2

Read the text once and then answer the questions below.

Philip and Sandra are from Germany. They arrived in Seattle yesterday to visit their American aunt Mary and uncle Richard. In their hotel they find two flyers, one about Pike Place Market and the other about the Seattle Center.

i ***Pike Place Market***

The country's oldest continuously operating open-air market, Pike Place Market, features area growers, bakers, fishmongers, artisans and street performers. The market is made up of several buildings. In the Main Arcade and the North Arcade you will find ***beautifully arranged foods***, ranging from potatoes to freshly caught fish and Asian delicacies. A must-see is the Flying Fish shop, where the sellers throw fish back and forth between each other until someone buys them. Downstairs, however, you will find a ***labyrinth of small shops*** that sell souvenirs, comics, books, toys, magicians' supplies, posters and anything else you can and cannot think of. You will find Pike Place Market at the Waterfront near the Aquarium. Go there to experience ***great shopping!***

Tick the correct answer.

Statement	true	false	not mentioned
a. Pike Place Market is a supermarket.			
b. Pike Place Market is expensive.			
c. Pike Place Market is a good place for tourists.			
d. Pike Place Market is a good place for people from Seattle.			
e. Pike Place Market is a good place for teenagers.			

3

Read the text once and then answer the questions below.

Seattle Center

Built for the World Fair in 1962, this exciting area of town is dominated by the **Space Needle**. This 605-foot-high tower offers **spectacular views** of downtown Seattle and the bay. The elevator zips you up into the restaurant in just 43 seconds. While you're enjoying a drink or a meal, the restaurant will revolve 360 degrees so you are able to look in all directions without having to move yourself. After looking at everything from above, enjoy the **attractions on the ground**: Fun Forest Amusement Park with its spectacular rides, the Seattle Opera House and two playhouses as well as two sports arenas. You can get to Seattle Center by **Monorail** from downtown or walk up from the Waterfront, it's just a five minute walk. Don't miss out on this **great part of town**.

Tick the correct answer.

Statement	true	false	not mentioned
a. Seattle Center is a zoo.			
b. Seattle Center offers many different kinds of activities.			
c. The most important building at Seattle Center is the Opera House.			
d. You can find a big wheel and a roller coaster at Seattle Center.			
e. You can see very far from the top of the Space Needle.			

9.2 Reading for detail and guessing words

4

Read the texts again. Can you guess the meaning of the words in the list? How did you guess?

After having read the flyers, Sandra and Philip are excited about these two places and want to tell Mary and Richard about them; but before they can do that they need to understand the details. They read the flyers again. Now they must guess the meanings of the words they don't know.

Word	Meaning	How did you guess?
fishmonger		
street performers		
delicacies		
magician		
spectacular		
to revolve		
to zip up		
waterfront		

5

Which words from the texts are missing here? Read the explanations and fill in the gaps.

There were a few other words they couldn't guess, so they went downstairs and asked the lady at the reception desk if she could help them.

Sandra: Excuse me, could you please help us with a few words?

Receptionist: Of course, young lady. Let's have a look at them.

Sandra: What are ______________________________?

Receptionist: Oh, these are farmers who have their farms near Seattle.

Philip: Thank you. And what about ______________________________?

Receptionist: They're people who make things with their hands – paintings, clothes, decorative or useful or beautiful things.

Sandra: Oh, of course. Now what's a ______________________________?

Receptionist: That's a place where you go to see plays being performed.

Philip: Thank you very much. One last question:
What's a ______________________________?

Receptionist: Well, it's something like a train, but it runs on only one rail, not on two rails.

Sandra: Thank you for your help. Good bye.

Receptionist: Anytime you have a question, please feel free to ask me.

6

Read the dialogue and then fill in the gaps using information from the texts.

Sandra and Philip have read all about the two places now, but they are still not sure where they should go. They ask two American teenagers they meet at the hotel.

Sandra: Hi, I'm Sandra from Germany, and this is my brother Philip. Could we ask you a question, please?

Marc: Sure, go ahead.

Philip: We've read these two flyers about Pike Place Market and Seattle Center, and we're not sure where we want to go. Which do you prefer?

Nancy: There's no question about it. Seattle Center is the best place. I loved the view from the ______________________________ and the ride on the ______________________________ – just 43 seconds – that's great.

Sandra: But isn't Pike Place Market fun, too – especially downstairs with all the ______________________________?

Marc: Yes, I agree. I like to do magic tricks and there's a great shop for ____.

Philip: I think so, too. I really like reading. I could buy ________________________ __________________. And I also want to see these crazy people who throw ______________________________ until someone buys them.

Nancy: Oh, forget about reading and flying fish. Seattle Center is so exciting. All the great ______________________________ at Fun Forest. I just loved them.

Sandra: Hmm, now what are we going to do?

Marc: It's easy. Just go to both places. They're both near the

________________________________ .

Philip: Yeah, that's a great idea. Do you think Richard and Mary will like that idea?

Sandra: Well, I'm not too sure about that. They probably want to take us to some art museum.

9.3 False friends

7

Draw lines connecting the false friends with each other. If you aren't quite sure, have a guess.
In the answer section you will find the correct answers, and the German translation for each of the false friends.

pickle	**cell phone**
football	**because**
bank	**boss**
stool	**bench**
gymnasium	**opinion**
handy	**soccer**
chef	**almost**
fast	**zit**
while	**high school**
meaning	**chair**

Now try to express the following actions in English. Don't translate!

a. Sage deinem Freund, dass er dich auf dem Handy anrufen soll.
Please call me on my cell phone.

b. Sage deinem Onkel, dass du zur Bank gehst.

___

c. Sage deiner Freundin, dass du mit den Hausaufgaben fast fertig bist.

___

d. Sage dem Kassierer im Supermarkt, dass du gerne mit seinem Chef reden möchtest.

___

e. Frage deinen Vater, ob er bitte deinen Stuhl reparieren könnte.

___

f. Bitte deinen Tischnachbarn, dir die sauren Gurken zu reichen.

___

Statt einen Test zu schreiben, beurteilst du deine Kenntnisse im Bereich Leseverstehen am besten selbst. Denke über die fünf Aussagen nach und kreuze dann erst an.

Aussage	**Klappt sehr gut**	**Gelingt mir manchmal**	**Muss ich weiter üben**
Ich kann die Hauptaussagen eines Textes beim ersten Lesen verstehen.			
Ich kann beim zweiten Lesen viele mir unbekannte Wörter erschließen.			
Nach Klärung des Vokabulars kann ich auch die Details eines Textes verstehen und festhalten.			
Ich kann die wichtigen Inhalte eines Textes selbst zusammenfassen und mit anderen darüber sprechen.			
Ich kenne schon viele *false friends* und mache wenig Fehler im Umgang mit ihnen.			

10 Listening comprehension

1 Check-up 25 – 26

Listen to what the people are saying – where are they?

1. 25

- [ ] On a plane approaching Chicago.
- [ ] On a plane approaching New York.
- [ ] On a cruise ship approaching New York.
- [ ] On a tour of Chicago's harbour.

2. 26

- [ ] On a bus.
- [ ] In a private car.
- [ ] In a taxi.
- [ ] On a motorcycle.

Dieses Kapitel kannst du auf drei Arten bearbeiten:

1 Du hörst immer nur einen Text und beantwortest nach dem ersten Hören die Fragen zum *Listening for gist* und nach dem zweiten Hören die zum *Listening for detail*.

2. Du hörst den ganzen Text am Stück und beantwortest nach dem ersten Hören die Fragen zum *Listening for gist* und nach dem zweiten Hören die zum *Listening for detail*. Dieser Weg ist natürlich deutlich schwieriger (vor allem beim *Listening for detail*).

3. Du bearbeitest das *Listening for gist* wie in 2 und das *Listening for detail* wie in 1.

Wenn du merkst, dass du den Text zum vollen Verständnis noch ein drittes Mal hören musst, kannst du das natürlich tun.

Beim *Listening for gist* solltest du dir die Fragen vorher nicht durchlesen, beim *Listening for detail* jedoch auf jeden Fall!

Hörverstehen

Hörverstehen bedeutet, viele Dinge gleichzeitig zu tun:

1. **Worte verstehen**
   Zunächst musst du natürlich die **Worte** verstehen und diejenigen, die du nicht verstehst, aus dem Zusammenhang erschließen.
2. **Geräusche erkennen**
   Geräusche helfen bei der Einordnung einer Situation, was das Verständnis des Gesagten erleichtert.
3. **Kulturelles Wissen anwenden**
   Manche Aussagen kann man nur verstehen, wenn man die Kultur des Sprechers kennt. Dazu gehören auch Dialekt oder Slang, so wie ihn der Taxifahrer im Check-up in Ansätzen gesprochen hat. Wenn die Gesprächspartner aus verschiedenen Kulturkreisen kommen, entstehen hier oft Missverständnisse.
4. **Wichtige Informationen von unwichtigen unterscheiden**
   Nicht alles, was gesagt wird, ist für dich wichtig. Du musst beim Zuhören also entscheiden, welche Information du wirklich brauchst und welche nicht.

Strategien für Hörverstehen

Dieses Kapitel übt verschiedene Aspekte des Hörverstehens getrennt. Im Check-up ging es darum, mit Hilfe von Geräusch und Rede herauszufinden, wo die Szene spielt. Oft kommen hier Wörter vor, die du nicht kennst. Das ist in einem fremden Land völlig normal und du sollst dich deshalb daran gewöhnen. Also keine Panik: Einfach weiterhören und versuchen, das Wort zu erraten – wenn es wichtig ist. In diesem Kapitel wirst du die folgenden Strategien üben:

1. ***Listening for gist:*** Das große Ganze ***(the gist)*** verstehen. In vielen Situationen ist das vollkommen ausreichend.
2. ***Intelligent guessing:*** Oft wird man durch Nebengeräusche gestört, oder man versteht einzelne Worte nicht. Diese Lücken lassen sich oft durch Nachdenken und Raten schließen oder man erkennt schnell, dass die Worte nicht wichtig sind.
3. ***Listening for detail:*** Nach Einzelheiten sucht man immer erst beim zweiten Hören. Oft schreibt man diese dann auch auf ***(taking notes)***. Wichtig hierbei ist, dass man nur Stichworte ***(key words)*** aufschreibt, da für ganze Sätze während des Zuhörens normalerweise keine Zeit ist.

10.1 Listening for gist

2 27 – 29

Listen to the radio and tick the correct answer. Sometimes more than one answer is correct.

27

1. The radio show is about …

☐ … theatre plays. ☐ … movie stars. ☐ … musicals.

28

2. The commercial is about …

☐ … tooth paste.
☐ … a lotion that helps against pimples* right away.
☐ … a lotion that cleans your skin.

*__pimple__ – Pickel

3. The boy in the commercial is in a panic because …

☐ … his girlfriend will break up with him if he has got a pimple on his face.
☐ … his friends will not like him any more if he has got a pimple on his face.
☐ … his mother will not let him go see a musical if he has got a pimple on his face.

29

4. How does the radio station show its listeners that musicals are interesting?

☐ They interview an actor from a musical.
☐ They interview teenagers whose parents have been to musicals.
☐ They interview teenagers who have seen musicals.
☐ They tell listeners about some musicals.
☐ They give away free tickets.
☐ They play music from a musical.

3 30 – 32

Listen to the three radio reports about the musicals. Choose the pictures that go with the musicals. Use **B** for "Beauty and the Beast"; **H** for "Little Shop of Horrors" and **M** for "Les Misérables". But be careful – some pictures don't go with any of the musicals!

4 33

Listen to the report on Broadway tickets. Tick those questions which are answered in the report.

- ☐ 1. Where can I buy Broadway tickets?
- ☐ 2. Can I order Broadway tickets before I get to New York?
- ☐ 3. What colour are the tickets?
- ☐ 4. How expensive are the tickets?
- ☐ 5. How can I get cheap tickets?
- ☐ 6. Is there a black market for tickets?
- ☐ 7. Why are some tickets cheaper than others?
- ☐ 8. Is it difficult to get tickets?
- ☐ 9. Do I need a credit card to buy them?

10.2 Listening for detail

5 30

Listen to the report on "Beauty and the Beast" once again. Then tick the correct answers – are they true, false, or not mentioned in the report?

	true	false	not mentioned
The enchanted prince looks like a beast until he finds a woman who takes him away.			
The prince's servants have also been enchanted to look like cups and other useful things.			
Belle had been looking for her horse when she found the castle.			
Belle likes the Beast from the beginning.			
The servants like Belle.			
Gaston likes Belle.			
The people of the village don't want to help Gaston attack the castle.			
Belle's father is afraid that Belle will be hurt.			
In the end the Beast dies in Belle's arms.			

6 31

Listen to the report on "Little Shop of Horrors" again and decide which of the following summaries is the best.

1. Seymour finds a strange flower that makes him and his shop famous and successful. He is in love with Audrey, who doesn't love him back, though. When Seymour finds out that his plant needs blood to survive he kills Audrey's boyfriend to feed the plant. When he finally finds out that the plant is a threat to the world he tries to destroy it but is eaten by it.

2. Seymour finds a strange flower that makes him and his shop famous and successful. He is also in love with Audrey, who doesn't love him back, though. When he finds out that Mr. Mushnik treats Audrey badly they fight and Seymour kills Mr. Mushnik by accident. Knowing that his plant needs blood, he feeds Mr. Mushnik to it. When Audrey and Seymour find out that the plant wants to kill all the animals on Earth, they decide to destroy it, but they fail and are eaten by the plant themselves.

3. Seymour is a poor man who finds a strange flower that makes him famous and his boss' shop successful. He is also in love with Audrey, who doesn't love him back, though. When he finds out that Mr. Mushnik treats Audrey badly they fight and Seymour accidentally kills Mr. Mushnik. Knowing that his plant needs blood, he feeds Mr. Mushnik to it. In the end Seymour and Audrey, who is now his girlfriend, find out that the plant wants to take over the world. When they try to stop it they are eaten themselves.

7 32

Listen to the report on "Les Misérables" again and put the sentences in the correct order by giving them numbers.

- ◯ Eponine dies while helping Marius.
- ◯ Jean Valjean decides to care for Cossette whose mother has died in a hospital.
- ◯ Jean Valjean becomes rich.
- ◯ Jean Valjean commits a crime again but is not caught and changes his name.
- ◯ All the dead appear on stage singing.
- ◯ Jean Valjean leaves prison after 19 years.
- ◯ Cossette grows up and falls in love.

8 33

Fill in the gaps in the following grid with information on Broadway tickets.

How to get Broadway tickets

… fast:

e ______________________

(up to $ ________)

… not so fast:

c ______________________

(starting at $ ________)

① A ______________ Rush Tickets 10 ______________ Tickets for $ ______

② Partial V __________ Tickets – most ______________ sell them

③ S ______________ Room ____________ Tickets for $ ________

④ W ______________ Matinee Tickets between $ ________ and $ ________ C ______________ than tickets for evening performances

disadvantages:

It's a lottery, so you ________ ______________ ______________ ______________.

Like it says – you might have to ______________ for the whole show!

The tickets may ____________ ______________ and you have to go ____________ ______________.

These aren't the best seats, so you don't ___ or ____________ everything.

Statt einen Test zu schreiben, beurteilst du deine Kenntnisse im Bereich Hörverstehen am besten selbst. Denke über die sechs Aussagen nach und kreuze dann erst an.

Aussage	Klappt sehr gut	Gelingt mir manchmal	Muss ich weiter üben
Ich kann nach einmaligem Hören Hauptaussagen einer Radiosendung verstehen.			
Ich kann Wichtiges von Unwichtigem nach einmaligem Hören unterscheiden.			
Ich kann gezielt Details aus einem Text heraushören.			
Ich kann nach dem zweiten Hören Detailfragen zum Text beantworten.			
Ich kann nach dem dritten Hören Detailfragen zum Text beantworten.			
Die Tatsache, dass ich einige Worte nicht verstehe, macht mich nicht besonders nervös. Ich kann sie erschließen oder erkenne, dass sie für mich nicht wichtig sind.			

Was ich bereits kann ...

Kreuze an, was für dich zutrifft.

	Kein Problem	Hier mache ich noch Fehler	Muss ich unbedingt noch üben
9 Reading comprehension			
1. Ich verstehe einen englischen Text beim ersten Lesen so, dass ich weiß, worum es darin geht.			
2. Ich kenne Techniken und Strategien, wie ich unbekannte Wörter in einem geschriebenen Text erschließen kann.			
3. Beim erneuten Lesen eines Textes bin ich in der Lage, auch Details zu verstehen.			
4. Ich weiß, was *false friends* sind, und kenne schon mindestens sechs.			
10 Listening comprehension			
5. Ich verstehe einen gesprochenen Text beim ersten Hören so, dass ich weiß, worum es darin geht.			
6. Ich kenne Techniken und Strategien, wie ich mir einen gesprochenen Text durch weiteres Hören erschließen kann.			
7. Ich gerate nicht in Panik, wenn ich gesprochene Wörter nicht sofort verstehe, sondern kann diese mit bestimmten Techniken erschließen oder erraten.			

Lösungen

1 The past perfect simple and progressive

1 Check-up

More than 20,000 years ago the first immigrants came to America across the Bering Strait. This was long after the first animals **had travelled** the same way looking for food. Yet, after Christopher Columbus **had discovered** America in 1492, life for the 1.5 million Native Americans, whom Columbus **had called** Indians, changed a lot. After news of the "New World" **had reached** Europe, thousands of people followed Columbus across the Atlantic to start a new life. Before the settlers from Europe came, most Native American tribes **had lived** nomadic lives. Now people with two different ways of life had to share the land, and that of course led to many conflicts. After Indians and Europeans **had fought** many wars and thousands of people **had died**, the Indians finally had to accept that they **had lost**. Of the 1.5 million Native Americans who **had lived** in America when Columbus arrived in 1492, only 350,000 remained in 1920. The nomads who 200 years earlier **had hunted** buffaloes now lived on reservations.

2

1. Fox had tried to think of a way to create fire **before** he decided to visit the geese.
2. **After** they had told him that they would teach him their cry, they gave him wings so he could fly with them.
3. But **before** they attached the wings, they had also told him never to open his eyes while flying.
4. The geese saw the village of the fireflies **after** darkness had come.
5. Fox had opened his eyes **before** he fell into the firefly village.

3

1. After two friendly fireflies **had come** to help fallen Fox, he **gave** each one of them a necklace of juniper berries.
2. After they **had lead** him to the cedar tree, they **explained** that it would catapult him over the wall if he wanted.
3. Fox **became** friends with the fireflies after he had **stayed** in the village for a few days.
4. Before the fireflies **helped** to gather wood to build a greater fire, they **had agreed** that a festival would be fun.
5. Fox **had tied** a piece of bark to his tail before he **built** a drum and **beat** a rhythm on it for the dancing flies.

6. After he **had started** to beat the drum, he **moved** slowly closer and closer to the fire.
7. He **had pretended** to tire from beating the drum before he **gave** the drum to some fireflies.
8. Before he **said**: "It's too warm here for me, I must find a cooler place," he **had held** his tail into the fire, lighting the bark.
9. After he **had started** running to the cedar tree, he **shouted**: "Bend down to me, my cedar tree, bend down!"

4

1. After Fox had landed on the other side, he started running. / Fox started running after he had landed on the other side. *or*
   Before Fox started running, he had landed on the other side. / Fox had landed on the other side before he started running.
2. After Fox had run past trees and bushes, they started to burn from the sparks dropping from the bark on his tail. / The trees and bushes started to burn from the sparks dropping from the bark on his tail after Fox had run past them.
   Die folgenden Versionen sind grammatikalisch richtig, aber schwer verständlich und nicht üblich.
   Before the trees and bushes started to burn from the sparks dropping from the bark on Fox's tail, Fox had run past them. / Fox had run past trees and bushes before they started to burn from the sparks dropping from the bark on his tail.
3. After Fox had become tired, he gave the bark to Hawk who carried it to brown Crane. / Fox gave the bark to Hawk who carried it to brown Crane after he had become tired. *or*
   Before Fox gave the bark to Hawk who carried it to brown Crane, he had become tired. / Fox had become tired before he gave the bark to Hawk who carried it to brown Crane.
4. After he had flown far to the south, dropping sparks everywhere, fires started burning all over the earth. / Fires started burning all over the earth after he had flown far to the south, dropping sparks everywhere. *or*
   Before fires started burning all over the earth, he had flown far to the south, dropping sparks everywhere. / He had flown far to the south, dropping sparks everywhere before fires started burning all over the earth.
5. After the fireflies had chased Fox all the way to his den, they said: "You will never be able to make use of the fire." / The fireflies said: "You will never be able to make use of the fire." after they had chased Fox all the way to his den. *or*
   Before the fireflies said: "You will never be able to make use of the fire.", they had chased Fox all the way to his den. / The fireflies had chased Fox all the way to his den before they said: "You will never be able to make use of the fire."

6. After the Apache nation had learned to control fire, they used it for cooking and to keep themselves warm in cold weather. / The Apache nation used fire for cooking and to keep themselves warm in cold weather after they had learned to control it. *or*
   Before the Apache nation used fire for cooking and to keep themselves warm in cold weather, they had learned to control it. / The Apache nation had learned to control fire before they used it for cooking and to keep themselves warm in cold weather.

5 Check-up

Before I left New York I **had been working** at a butcher's since 1846, when I had arrived in the New World. It was terrible. When I got up in the mornings at 4 o'clock, I had only slept for 5 hours, because we **had been working** from 6 o'clock a.m. until 8 o'clock p.m. every day, and I had a long way to go to get to work. I **had been doing** this for two years when I decided that I had to get away. In that time I received a letter from a friend who **had been living** in California for two years. He wrote that he had just found gold. So I decided to take my chances, too. I **had been saving** money for some time so that I had enough to start the trip. But now I'm in the middle of the wilderness and I'm starting to think that the butcher's in New York wasn't so bad after all …

6 1

Talk on the trail

1. *Phil:* You look very tired, Sue.
   Sue: Yes, I had only slept for two hours when the trumpet was blown.
   Phil: Why was that?
   Sue: I **had been dreaming** of attacking Indians and couldn't go back to sleep afterwards.
2. *Alex:* Did you check on the cattle last night?
   Joe: Yeah, they **had been grazing** peacefully since we left them but they were a little nervous later on. There might have been a bear out there.
3. Marie: We're late starting this morning, mom.
   Mrs. Morris: I told you, it's because the men **had been scouting** more carefully. They thought that there might have been some Indians out there.
4. *Phil:* I've just come back from hunting. What happened to Mitchell?
   Alex: He had just found the fresh water he **had been** / he**'d been looking** for all morning when a puma appeared and attacked him. Mitchell and the puma

had been fighting for a few minutes already when Joe came just in time to save Mitchell's life. How about you, did you shoot anything?

Phil: No, I **had been / I'd been following** a herd of buffaloes for three hours when they saw me and ran away.

7

Mick Mitchell's diary after the trip

We have finally made it. It was terrible. After we **had left** New York, everything seemed to be fine. But then many crazy things happened. One morning I woke up and saw that it **had been raining** all night. However, it **had** just **stopped**, so I jumped out of the wagon and realized that it was almost impossible to walk because of all the mud. We also quickly realized that it would be difficult to move the wagons. We were only able to move again after we **had been pushing** and **pulling** for three hours. We also had to shoot a cow that **had broken** its leg. It **had been trying** to get out of a big puddle when it somehow tripped, fell and hurt itself. A few days later I was attacked by a puma because I **hadn't been** careful enough. I **had been looking** for water when it suddenly appeared out of the woods. I **had been fighting** the puma with my bare hands for a few minutes when Joe came and shot it. I am really happy to be in my new home now: California!

8

How Mick Mitchell left California

After Mick **had been looking for gold for about three months without success**, he decided to give up. He had to realise that all the good claims had been taken by other diggers already. **While he was sitting next to the river, thinking how life might go on,** a rich-looking man started talking to him. He wanted to know **what Mick had been doing for the past few years.** So Mick told him his story, and **while he was talking,** the man became more and more interested. **The rich man was looking for strong men** who had already travelled the Oregon trail. **He had been digging for gold for only a few weeks** and now wanted to take his gold back to New York. However, he needed men to protect him from robbers. Mick decided to accept the job because the man promised him a lot of money. When Mick arrived in New York **after he'd been travelling in the wilderness for two years,** he had to find work with a butcher once again. The rich man had never paid him, and was never heard of again.

Test

1

The story of Pocahontas

1. Pocahontas was still a child when the first settlers **arrived** in Virginia.
2. Pocahontas had always **been** a very curious child and therefore she wanted to get to know these strange white people.
3. After Pocahontas **had** saved the life of an English prisoner, the settlers started to like her.
4. Before she **married** an English colonist, she had become a Christian.
5. The relationship between the English and Pocahontas' tribe **became** more peaceful after she had married a colonist.

2

After Pocahontas **had learned** the English language she **made** friends among the settlers. However, when war **broke** out between the settlers and Pocahontas' tribe, she was taken prisoner. When her father **refused** to pay ransom for her, the English **kept** her prisoner, but **treated** her well. She **had been living** in Jamestown as a prisoner for a few months when she **decided** to get baptised and to marry a settler called John Rolf. This marriage **stopped** the war between the Europeans and the Indians that **had been going** on for almost a year. Some time later, after she **had had** a baby, whom she **had named** Thomas, she **travelled** to England with her husband. Unfortunately though, Rebecca, which was now her name, **died** in England after she **became** ill. She was only 22 years old, but she **had done** a lot to bring the two peoples together.

Conditional sentences 2

1 Check-up

	I	II	III
What would you do if you saw a black bear?		x	
If I saw a black bear, I would stay calm and think, "Wow, this is really cool!"		x	
If you meet a bear, there are several things that might happen.	x		
If the bear sees you, it will usually leave, because it doesn't care much about people.	x		
Bears sometimes start running towards you if they feel threatened.	x		
If this happens, just talk softly to the bear and walk slowly backwards.	x		
Never run away! Many accidents would not have happened if people hadn't run away from a bear.			x

2

Rules and Regulations in Death Valley National Park

1. If we want Death Valley to remain a nice, safe and clean place, every visitor must follow some rules.
2. Animal and plant life will be damaged if you leave the roads with your car or motorcycle.
3. If you own a gun, we ask you kindly not to bring it. Hunting is strictly forbidden.
4. Please use the fire pits in the official campgrounds if you want to make a fire.
5. If you are planning to camp in the park, please see the Rangers at Furnace Creek Visitor Center and ask them about campsites.
6. Wild animals might become ill or even die if you feed them.

3

1. If you break/violate the rules/regulations, you will have to pay a fine.
2. If too many people break/violate the rules, they will be made stricter/harsher/ more severe.
3. Please be extra/especially careful if/when you travel with children.

4

At a campground in Yosemite National Park

- If it wasn't raining, Melissa would go hiking. / Melissa would go hiking if it wasn't raining.
- If Abigail's car wasn't broken, she would drive home today. / Abigail would drive home today if her car wasn't broken.
- If Mike's bottle wasn't empty, he would drink some water. / Mike would drink some water if his bottle wasn't empty.
- If Martha wasn't sleeping / asleep, she would watch the sunset. / Martha would watch the sunset if she wasn't sleeping / asleep.
- If Kyle had a mountain bike, he would go biking. / Kyle would go biking if he had a mountain bike.

5

1. If I had a tent, I would sleep in the wilderness.
2. If I slept in the wilderness, I would see many animals.
3. I would be very happy/pleased if I saw a bear.

6

Everything could have been different

1. The truck wouldn't have got stuck if the road hadn't been so muddy.
2. If the truck hadn't got stuck, he would have stayed inside it.
3. He might not have seen the cub if he hadn't got out of the car.
4. If he hadn't got out of the car, mama-bear might not have seen him.
5. If she hadn't seen him, she would not have charged at him.
6. He would have run away if he hadn't been stuck in the mud.
7. He might have been killed if he had run away.
8. If the bear hadn't roared right in his face, he would not have smelled its breath.
9. He would not have had nightmares for weeks if all this hadn't happened.

7

Great lies about bear encounters

1. If I hadn't had a ball, the two cubs would not have played soccer with me.
2. If I hadn't started singing a lullaby, the bear would have killed me.
3. If the bear hadn't lost its glasses, it would have seen me.
4. I wouldn't have been able to kill the bear if I hadn't brought my pocket knife.
5. The bear wouldn't have started singing if I hadn't given it a glass of whisky.
6. If I had taken a shower during the last week, the bear wouldn't have run away from me.

8

1. If I had seen a bear, I would have been afraid/scared.
2. The bear might have attacked if it had realized that I was afraid.
3. If it had attacked me, I would have run away.
4. If I had run away, it might have killed me.

9

A trip to Yosemite

- If we go hiking in Yosemite, we will see a lot of animals.
- If we had taken a map with us, we wouldn't have lost the way.
- Alex would come with us to Yosemite if he didn't have to go to summer school.
- If Alex hadn't been so lazy throughout the school year, he could have come with us to Yosemite.
- We will rent a tent if we go on an overnight trip.
- I would climb El Capitano if I was a better climber.
- If we had got up earlier, we could have seen the beautiful sunrise.
- If we don't pitch the tent soon, we will get very wet.
- We wouldn't have gotten so wet if we had pitched the tent sooner.
- If we caught a fish, I would cook it for dinner.

10 2

Jenny: If we **walk** tomorrow as far as we did today, I **will die**.

Andrea: I agree, Jenny – but it **wouldn't have been** so bad if Bill **hadn't lost** the map.

Bill: That's not fair! If you **had put** it in my backpack after the break, I **wouldn't have lost** it.

John: You know, I think we should worry about the weather. If it **wasn't raining**, we **could sit** outside now and watch the stars.

Andrea: Oh John, you're so romantic. If we **didn't have** you with us, we **might/would forget** about the beauty of nature altogether.

John: That's right. And if you **weren't** here, nobody **would make** smart comments all the time.

Jenny: Well, if I ever **return** home, I **will take** a long, hot bath and afterwards I **will look** at the stars – if it **doesn't rain**, of course.

John: Ha, ha. If I **survive** this trip, I **will write** a book about it.

Test

1

The following options are correct:

1. If you want to take a rafting trip through the Grand Canyon, you **must take (would have to take)** a bus ride to Diamond Creek.
2. Groups of teenagers will only be admitted if they **bring (brought)** an adult.
3. If people **didn't fall (hadn't fallen)** into the water very often on these trips, they wouldn't be so popular.
4. If people aren't careful, they **will be hurt / might be hurt**.
5. "If I **hadn't gone**, I would have regretted it afterwards," one guest said last week.
6. If more people **went on** this trip, they would understand how beautiful the world is.
7. People **wouldn't treat / might not treat** the environment as badly if they realized how beautiful the world is.

2

If you **travel / are travelling** from one National Park to the next, you have to plan your trip carefully. You have to make sure that your car is in good shape. If it **breaks** down somewhere in the desert between two parks, it **will be / might be / could be** difficult to get help quickly. It **is** also important to take enough water with you if you drive through the deserts of Nevada. A friend of mine told me recently: "If I **hadn't taken** extra water with me last summer, I'd be dead now." He had been stuck in the desert with a flat tire for two days.

You should also take a good tent and a warm sleeping bag with you. "If only the nights weren't so cold, travelling the National Parks **would be / could be** much more comfortable," my husband said when we woke up and found frozen puddles in front of our tent in Montana. "Well," I answered, "if you **had bought** yourself a good sleeping bag, you wouldn't mind so much." He was quite mad at me then and said: "I would have bought a better sleeping bag if you **hadn't spent** all our money on the camping stove - and if you don't get out of your beautifully warm sleeping bag right now and make some coffee, I **will pack** my bags and go home." So the end of the story is: if I **hadn't brought** the coffee, my vacation would have been over right then."

3

1. If America didn't have so many National Parks, not so many people would go there on vacation. *or*
   Not so many people would go there on vacation if America didn't have so many National Parks.
2. If people like the National Parks, they will protect / might protect the environment more actively. *or*
   If people liked the National Parks, they would protect / might protect the environment more actively.
3. I wouldn't have enjoyed my last vacation if I hadn't visited the Grand Canyon.
   or
   If I hadn't visited the Grand Canyon, I wouldn't have enjoyed my last vacation.

Relative clauses 3

1 Check-up

- Cheerleaders are a group of girls who / that try to help our sports teams during the games.
- A Wolverine is an animal that / which lives in the woods, but it's also our school's mascot.
- The yearbook team is a group of students who / that write a book about the school year.
- A task is something that / which must be done.
- A choir is a group of students who / that sing together.
- A rehearsal is a kind of practice that / which performers do to learn their parts.

2

Pocket money

How much pocket money should a teenager get **who / that** is 16 years old and still living at home? Parents **who / that** earn a lot of money often don't think enough about this question, and give their kids as much as they ask for. Their children are the ones **who / that** come to school with expensive new electronic devices **which / that** they have bought "just like that" on their way to school. In contrast, the parents **whose** children have very little money are often the ones **who / that** think that they are behaving more responsibly. They think that children **who / that** still go to school are too young to make important decisions about money, and should learn to live with just a little bit of money. But of course the kids **who / that** do not have a lot of pocket money have serious problems, because they have to compete with their classmates **whose** pockets are stuffed with money. We believe that pocket money is one of the reasons **which / that** make life difficult for many of us.

What do you think about pocket money? Tick your answer!

	agree	don't agree
Only students **who / that** get at least $20 a week should be allowed to come to Bismarck High.		
The student government should decide on the amount of money **that / which** students are allowed to bring to school.		
A student's pocket money and what he or she does with it is not a matter **that / which** the school should be interested in.		
The principal should talk to the parents **who / that** give their children too much money.		

3

Should teenagers work for their money?

We have interviewed people **we met in the streets** and collected their opinions. Here they are:

Older lady: I believe that teenagers **who work for their money** don't have enough time to work for school. I also believe that parents **whose children work** are not responsible parents.

Little boy: My brother works at the ice-cream parlor downtown. I think that was the best idea **he ever had** because I always get ice-cream for free.

Owner of ice-cream parlor: Teenagers are good cheap workers. The amount of ice-cream **I have sold since I started employing teenagers** has risen quite a bit. But the number of friends **they give the ice-cream for free** is also quite large.

Mother of two teenagers: Working with your own two hands is one of the experiences **every person should make sooner or later**. I believe that money **that was earned by hard work** will be spent responsibly. Both of my children work.

School teacher: Teenagers **who have never had a job during their school time** miss an important experience. However, the teenagers' most important job is school. Jobs **that keep students from doing their homework** should be forbidden by responsible parents.

What's your opinion on teenage work?

	that's right	no way
Teenagers **who get bad marks at school** should ask their teacher before they start a job.		
Parents **who allow their kids to work at nights** should be punished.		
Jobs **the teenagers do to help the family to pay for food and rent** are absolutely OK, even if the kids get bad marks.		
It must be the teenagers themselves **who decide if they want to work or not**. It's nobody else's business.		

4 Check-up

	important	extra information
Mr. Cohen, who is eighty years old, thinks that today's teenagers watch too much TV.		c
Philip thinks that TV shows that teach teenagers something are very helpful.	o	
Many people believe that the internet, which is used by millions of people every day, has been one of the greatest inventions of the last century.		m
MP3 players can contain a lot more music than a disc-man could, which is very useful if you are away from home for a long time.		m
A digital camera is a camera that takes photos without needing a film.	a	

Solution: A very important part of a non-defining relative clause is the **comma**.

5

Internet addiction

	def.	extra
Using the internet is a hobby that may cost families a lot of money.	x	
Especially if the teenagers spend a lot of time on pay sites, which are usually made to trick their users anyway.		x
Many of theses pay sites, which make their owners rich and their users poor, are gaming sites.		x
The real problems arise when teenagers, whose parents often find out too late about their hobby, become addicted to their game.		x
Even if their parents take their computers away from them it doesn't change anything for the teenagers who then just go to internet cafes to go online.	x	
Psychologists say that internet-addiction is a problem that is almost as serious as drug-addiction.	x	
However, they say that there are at least as many internet-addicts among grown-ups as among teenagers, which is not really surprising because they have enough money to finance it.		x
For those addicts who want to solve the problem it is important to accept that there is a problem.	x	
Once they have done that, they can look for a psychiatrist who is specialised in internet addiction.	x	

6

1. His father**, who works for a TV company,** thinks that this is normal for a teenager.
2. His mother**, who is a housewife,** believes that Marc watches too much TV.
3. She has talked to other parents from Marc's school**, whose name / the name of which is Glenwood Springs High School,** and they all agreed with her.
4. She also tried to tell him to go and spend more time outside with his friends**, who play a lot of soccer**.
5. But Marc told her that he didn't have any friends and that he would much rather keep on watching his favourite show**, which is called "The Simpsons"**.
6. When she heard this she started to cry and screamed at Marc**, who just sat there and didn't understand what her problem was**.
7. At that moment she woke up from her nap**, which she had taken in the garden,** and saw Marc walking out of the house with his tennis-racket in his hand.

7

Another daydream

	word	sentence
Our school has a new computer lab which was installed this summer.	x	
The teachers are now looking for a group of pupils which want to look after the room during the breaks.	x	
My best friend wants to join the group, which is really good for me, because then he can show me everything.		x
You know, I'm really bad with computers, which is something I want to change.		x
If he helps me, I will soon be able to join the computer club, which is the coolest club at school.		x
That's because the members of the computer club can always help other students with their computer problems, which makes them very popular.		x

8

Internet crime

1. Others copy thousands of CDs and sell them, **which is an easy way to earn money.**
2. The companies who sell the music are of course angry with these people, **which is quite understandable.**
3. Finally, more and more governments have passed laws punishing such behaviour, **which has of course not made everybody happy.**
4. The people who have illegally copied music are afraid of going to jail, **which shows that the laws might be quite successful.**
5. Yet most music companies think that the punishments should be much greater, **which shows that many people are still copying music illegally.**

Test

1

If you're designing a website **which / that** is aimed at teenagers, you'd better not make the fonts too small. That's not because teens have bad eyes, but because teenagers **who / that** sit in front of their computers tend to lean back in their chairs.

This advice and much more for people **who / that** want to create websites for teens can be found in a new book by Jakob Nielsen. Since three quarters of all American teens are web users, people **whose** job it is to get teenagers to use the internet should be very interested in this book**, which** is already a bestseller.
"It's interactivity **which / that** makes the difference. That's what all teenagers are looking for," says Nielsen**, who** prepared for the study by observing American and Australian teenagers using dozens of websites. They want to be doing something, "as opposed to just sitting and reading**, which** they think is boring. Apart from that, they say that reading is something **which / that** they do enough of already in school." The best interactive elements include message boards, polls, quizzes, being able to ask questions of experts, and tools **which / that** let teens construct their own web pages.
Another element teens find attractive is the use of photographs and images **which** make texts easier to understand. Teens are much less willing than adults to spend time on websites **which / that** have a lot of good information but are no fun to look at." Adults**, who / that** might need the information for their work**,** are more willing to read long texts without pictures or animations.

2

In his book Nielsen names some sites **that teenagers like**. One is *SparkNotes***, which offers study guides on subjects from math to chemistry**. He explains that the teens **who took part in his study** enjoyed the site's combination of useful information, good design and interactivity. The other part of the site **which they liked** was its interface**, which made it easy for them to find what they needed to do their homework**.
CSUMentor and *TeensHealth* were other sites **which the teenagers liked** because they smartly mix information and presentation and don't ask teens to work too hard**, which seems to show that teens who surf the net might be just a little bit lazy**.

Rewritten

In his book Nielsen names some sites **teenagers like**.
The other part of the site **they liked** was its interface, which made it easy for them to find what they needed to do their homework.
CSUMentor and *TeensHealth* were other sites **the teenagers liked** because they smartly mix information and presentation and don't ask teens to work too hard, which seems to show that teens who surf the net might be just a little bit lazy.

Talking about the future 4

1 Check-up

Mr. Adams: Mr. and Mrs. Schuster and their twins Kai and Sophie are going to visit us this summer. **(3)**
I believe you will like their children a lot. **(4)**
Mrs. Adams: Mrs. Schuster is also a teacher, so she is going to visit our school. **(3)**
Don't worry, Jennifer. Their plane back to Germany leaves on July 6th. **(1)**
They won't interfere with your trip to Montana. **(4)**
Ken: Great! We'll show them Chicago. **(4)**
I'll get some brochures for tourists. **(4)**
Jennifer: That's not a good idea. I'm visiting friends in Montana this summer. **(2)**
Summer vacation starts on July 26th. **(1)**

2 3

1. *Ken:* Well, Mum and Dad, we've actually worked out a really good plan. First, we**'re/are going to take** Kai and Sophie to Sears Tower Skydeck to give them a view over the city. We**'re/are not going to do** a guided tour of Chicago, though. We both think that's boring. Instead Kai and Sophie**'re/are going to experience** Chicago together with us.
2. *Jennifer:* I**'m/am going to show** them the most interesting places and Ken**'s/is going to explain** baseball to them. We**'re/are also going to watch** a game.
3. *Mr. Adams:* Which team **are you going to watch**, the Cubs or the White Sox?
4. *Ken:* The Chicago White Sox, of course. They**'re/are going to get to know** a real team, not just losers!
5. *Jennifer:* I**'m/am going to go** to Navy Pier with them. And we**'re/are going to have a look at** the sharks at the Shedd Aquarium.
   Ken: Those are our ideas so far.
   Mr. Adams: That sounds good.

3 4

1. *Mrs. Adams:* But don't you think that the weather**'ll/will be** great for a boat tour on the Chicago River?
2. *Jennifer:* I guess Sophie**'ll/will prefer** to go shopping. That's more interesting.
3. *Ken:* I'm sure that we**'ll/will find** something interesting for everybody.
4. *Mr. Adams:* We just hope you**'ll/ will** all **enjoy** yourselves. You don't need to show them everything. Just have fun.
5. *Mrs. Adams:* But they should do something more than just shopping and baseball. What **will** their parents **say** if their children get the impression that Chicago is just a big shopping mall?

6. *Mr. Adams:* Not to forget all the baseball! You heard it children. You**'ll/will need to add** some more cultural highlights.
7. *Jennifer:* The chance that I **won't survive** this visit has just reached 80 per cent.

4 5

1. *Ken:* So what **are you going to do** on your first day here?
2. *Kai:* I**'m/am going to sleep** a lot. I'm so tired.
3. *Sophie:* I**'m/am going to unpack** my suitcase. But I think I**'ll/will have to help** my mother do some shopping, too.
4. *Jennifer:* That's just like in our family. I also have to do the shopping for my lazy brother. I**'ll/will help** you, Sophie.
5. *Ken:* Thanks, Jenny. You're so charming. I think I**'ll/will help** Mum and Dad. It looks as if we**'re/are going to have** a barbecue this evening. Well, the weather is great for it.
6. *Jennifer:* I guess Leslie and Brian **won't be** around tonight. But Antonio is here. Could you give him a call?
7. *Ken:* No problem. I**'ll/will call** him. Perhaps he can come.

5

2. *Jennifer:* Brian and Leslie are meeting us at the Sears Tower at 1 pm.
3. *Brian:* How long are you staying?
4. *Sophie:* The museum closes at 4 pm.
5. *Jennifer:* We're/We are taking the bus at 8.30 pm.
6. *Ken:* The bus leaves in 10 minutes.

6 6

1. *Ken:* Oh no, it's 8:25 already … We**'ll/will probably miss** the bus that **leaves** at 8:30 from the station, and **we'll/will be late / we're/we are going to be late** for dinner. Mom **will not / won't be happy** about that.
2. *Jennifer:* Let's check when the other buses **run**. Who's got the plan ?
3. *Brian:* I've got it. Let's see. Number six **leaves** at 8:35. Do you think **we'll/will be able to make** that?
4. *Sophie:* Don't worry, I**'m/am going to run** the Berlin Marathon in September. I can run for quite a while.
5. *Leslie:* You**'re/are going to take part** in a marathon? Cool!
6. *Brian:* Well, then, let's run and let's see **who'll/will be** first …

Test

1 7

1. *Ken:* **Are you really going to fly** to the West Coast tomorrow? That's sad.
2. *Kai:* Yes. But we don't want to. We**'re/We are not going to go**. Sophie and I have changed our plans. We want to stay here.
3. *Sophie:* And how **are you going to convince** our parents?
4. *Kai:* I**'m/**I **am just going to tell** them to pick us up here in Chicago on their way back to Germany.
5. *Jennifer:* Good idea. Our parents really like you. I'm sure they**'re/are going to let you stay** here for two more weeks.

2 8

1. *Jennifer:* I**'ll/will miss** you, Sophie.
2. *Sophie:* Can't we stay for two more weeks, mum? The rest of our trip **will not/ won't be** as good as Chicago anyway.
3. *Kai:* Yes, why don't you leave us here and pick us up on the way back? We**'ll/will help** Mr. and Mrs. Adams in the house.
4. *Mrs. Schuster:* No, I'm sorry children. That's not possible. But perhaps the Adams family **will come** to Germany one day.
5. *Mrs. Adams:* That sounds great. We**'ll/will think** about it.

3 9

1. *Jennifer:* Oh mom, please. Let us visit them in Germany. It **'ll/will be** so much fun.
2. *Mrs. Adams:* Well, it's not that easy. We**'ll/will have to think** about a lot of things before we can make such a big decision.
3. *Mr. Adams:* For example, who**'s/is going to mess up** your room when you're away, Jen? I mean, somebody has to do it.
   Jennifer: Dad! I'm serious.
4. *Mrs. Adams:* Well, one important point is the summer vacation. When **does it start** in Germany next year?
5. *Mrs. Schuster:* I'm not quite sure. Sometime at the beginning of August. Wait a second, I**'ll/will look it up**. It's August 3rd.
6. *Mrs. Adams:* Well, we**'re/are having** a big family meeting in Boston the week before, but after that it's all right.
7. *Jennifer:* Really, mom? That's fantastic. I**'m/am really going to go** to Germany.
8. *Sophie:* And we**'re/are going to show** you Munich. You**'ll/will see/'re/are going to see** the German Museum, the English Garden and …

5 Modal auxiliaries and their replacements

1 Check-up

At school

Which question is more polite?

- [x] May I go to the bathroom?
- [ ] Can I go to the bathroom?

Which teacher is more serious?

- [ ] You can't talk in class!
- [x] You mustn't talk in class!

Which student is more sure about what he can see?

- [x] The man in the picture could be an Indian.
- [ ] The man in the picture might be an Indian.

In which sentence does the teacher tell the students that the homework is not really important?

- [x] You needn't do this homework.
- [ ] You shouldn't do this homework.

You want to tell your friends that you can't come to the party because your parents don't want you to. What do you say?

- [ ] I'm not able to come to the party tonight.
- [x] I'm not allowed to come to the party tonight.

How do you say "I must do my homework" using the simple past?

- [ ] I must do my homework.
- [x] I had to do my homework.

How do you say "I can't go to school because I'm ill" using the will-future?

- [ ] I will can't go to school because I'm ill.
- [x] I won't be able to go to school because I'm ill.

2

1. Can you play football?
2. May we eat during class?
3. Are we allowed to chew gum during class tests?
4. May we ask our parents for help when we don't know how to do our homework?
5. May I go to the bathroom?

3

1. Students aren't allowed to come to school whenever they want to.
2. Teachers don't have to / needn't give good marks for every class test.

3. Students may not talk during class as much as they want.
4. Teachers don't have to / needn't cook lunch for the students every day.
5. Students aren't allowed to listen to music during the lessons.

4

1. May I go home, please?
2. Can I have your pen, please?
3. Could you help me with this maths exercise, please?
4. Can I copy your homework, please?
5. May I answer the question, please?

5

Hier hängt deine Antwort davon ab, wie sicher du bist, das erkannt zu haben, was dargestellt ist. Die Lösungen hier sind Vorschläge.

1. This **is** a playground / schoolyard.
2. This **may** be a teacher.
3. This **could** be a book.
4. This **might** be a pen.
5. This **is** a [school] bag.
6. This **could** be a TV.

6

1. *Mother:* You **have to** work harder for Spanish, Mary.
2. *Teacher:* I think you **have to** go home and see a doctor, Simon.
3. *Teacher (to himself):* I **must** find a new job.
4. *Student:* Why doesn't anybody do something? Someone **has to** call a doctor!
5. *Neighbour:* I think you **should** wake up, Stan.

7

1. Students must raise their hand before speaking.
2. Students should listen to each other.
3. Everyone ought to cooperate with their/his/her group.
4. Everyone ought to leave other people's materials alone.
5. Class members may not interrupt other students' learning.
6. Students may not write or carve on their desk or other school property.
7. Everybody must treat computers with care.
8. Absolutely no one is allowed to eat gum, candy or other food.
9. Everyone ought to be organized and prepared for class.

8

1. Students **will have to** raise their hand before speaking.
2. Students **were supposed to** listen to each other.
3. Everyone **had been supposed to** cooperate with their / his / her group.
4. Everyone **was supposed to** leave other people's materials alone.
5. Class members **will not be allowed to** interrupt other students' learning.
6. Students **will not be allowed to** write or carve on their desk or other school property.
7. Everybody **has had to** treat computers with care.
8. Absolutely no one **will be allowed to** eat gum, candy or other food.
9. Everyone **had been supposed to** be organized and prepared for class.

9 10

Mr. Mathews: Good morning, class. I have corrected your class tests and I **couldn't / wasn't able to** find a single good one. What went wrong? I **must / have to** admit, I was quite surprised and at the same time very sad. We really **have to / must** talk about this. I **cannot / can't** believe that you didn't understand anything I have been trying to teach you. Maybe I **should / ought to** look for a new job. But **may** I ask you a question before I do this? How many of you think they didn't practice enough for this test? What – all of you? Oh, so it wasn't all my fault. You really **must / have to** prepare better for the tests if you want to get good grades. **Shall** I talk to your parents about this? No? None of you want me to talk to your parents? OK, then we have to make a deal: you promise to work harder in this class, and I won't tell your parents about this disaster.

After class the students are talking to each other:

Alice: My parents will kill me if they find out about this test! But I'm so bad at Spanish. I think I **need** extra help.

Margaret: But then you **should** tell your parents about the test. If you don't tell them, they **cannot / can't** know that you're having problems learning Spanish.

Joe: Oh come on, I think the test was too difficult anyway. I think Mathews **ought to / should** make the tests easier. We are such a nice class.

Claire: Well, he **may / might** make the next test easier if we give him a little present.

Arthur: Oh, come on – you know he **isn't allowed to** do that. He would lose his job.

Alice: Hmm, sounds like I **may** be killed this afternoon. See you in heaven. Do they have Spanish tests there?

Test

1

1.	may	to be allowed to	**must**	might
2.	must	**might**	have to	should
3.	**ought to**	may	could	might
4.	should	ought to	**could**	shall

2

I'm very late for class.
- I must hurry. ☒
- I needn't hurry. ☐

You look tired.
- Yes, I really need to sleep more. ☒
- Yes, I ought to get up earlier. ☐

She looks really unhappy.
- Yes, she needs to work harder for school. ☐
- Yes, she might have done badly in another bad test. ☒

Pete is very bad in English. If he fails the test, he will have to leave school.
- Pete needn't pass the test. ☐
- Pete must pass the test. ☒

3 11

Alice is afraid of the next class test.
Joe: Hi Alice. I thought you were dead.
Alice: Well, my parents let me live. I **had to** promise to get better in Spanish, though. **Could** you *please* help me?
Joe: What do you want me to do?
Alice: You **could** sit next to me next time.
Joe: You really **mustn't** look at me like that. I **may / might** fall in love with you and then I **may / might** do stupid things.
Alice: Oh Joey, I'll be lost without you. I **need** your help or I'll be lost forever.
Joe: Maybe I **could** just help you prepare for the next test.
Alice: But what if that doesn't help? Oh Joey, what **shall / should** I do?
Joe: First of all you **must / have to** relax. Spanish isn't the only thing in the world. You really **should / ought to** think of other things. For example the new movie at the cinema. You **must / have to** see it, it's great.
Alice: **Could** you please be serious?
Joe: No, I **can't**, I'm in love with a girl that **can't** speak Spanish.

6 Reported speech

1 Check-up

direct speech	reported speech
1. "I may come back very late tonight."	c. *Christopher:* "A girl in a dress said that she might come back very late that night."
2. "Can I have the keys to my room, please!"	f. *Erica:* "A drunk guy asked the receptionist to give him the keys to his room."
3. "Have you ever travelled alone?"	h. *Erica:* "A girl with red hair asked someone whether she had ever travelled alone."
4. "I like long bus rides."	a. *Christopher:* "A little boy told someone that he liked long bus rides."
5. "My parents will take me to Hawaii next summer."	e. *Christopher:* "A young girl said her parents would take her to Hawaii the following summer."
6. "I spent last winter in Europe with my friends."	b. *Erica:* "An older traveller mentioned that he had spent the previous winter in Europe with his friends."
7. "When does the next bus to New York leave?"	d. *Erica:* "A backpacker asked his friend when the next bus to New York left."
8. "I'm going to stay in the cheapest hotel in Manhattan."	i. *Christopher:* "Another very dirty-looking guy said that he was going to stay in the cheapest hotel in Manhattan."
9. "Don't tell my girlfriend that I went out late."	g. *Christopher:* "A good-looking teenager told his friend not to tell his girlfriend that he had gone out late."

2 12

Christopher: Well, Erik explained that **it was a long way to travel**, but Pete said that **Las Vegas was great**.

Erica: That's right, but Kyle told us **that New Orleans wasn't a good place to go** because it **was too far south**. Yes, hmmm, and Connie, oh yes, she thought **Mesa Verde was interesting** because **we could see the Indian cave-dwellings**.

Christopher: You know, I think Suzanne is not very good at geography. She told me that **Florida was beautiful** because **we could go swimming there**. Doesn't she know where Florida is?

Erica: Well, let's forget about this. Marianne told us **not to go to Kansas** because **it was boring**. I think that's good to know.

Christopher: You're right. And Joey said **that the Great Lakes were fun**. Maybe we can go swimming there.

Anna: So where will we go? I'll go to a travel agency and find out more tomorrow.

3

Anna's mother **thought** that it was a great idea to travel through America, but she also **told** them to be very careful.
Anna's father was very excited and **explained / said** that he had done a trip like that 30 years before.
However, he also **asked / told** them to be careful, especially in the Alaskan wilderness.
Anna laughed and **explained / said** that they weren't planning on going to Alaska, so he could relax.
Her father **thought / believed** that that was a good idea. He **wanted to know / wondered** where they were planning on going instead.
Anna **said / answered** that they hadn't made any plans.
Her father was very excited and he **told** her to visit a hundred wonderful places.
Half an hour later, Anna put down the phone and was very confused about her trip.
Then she wrote to her grandmother. She answered quickly, and in her letter she **told** Anna that she was too young for such a trip and that she should rather stay at home.
She also **said** that America was too far away.
She **told / asked** her to come home as fast as possible.
She also **believed / wrote** that America was full of gangsters and was a really dangerous place.
In the end she **warned / told / asked** Anna not to leave the house until her father could come and bring her back home.
When she showed this letter to Christopher and Erica they laughed. They **said / thought** that grandparents were the same all over the world.

4 13

Die einleitenden Frageverben sind frei austauschbar.

Erica: What did you find out, Anna?

Anna: Not much really. The lady just asked a lot of questions and when I couldn't answer some of them, she told me to go home, find out, and then come back.

Christopher: Alright. What did she ask?

Anna: First she **asked if we were old enough to travel alone (1)**.

When I said "yes", she **wondered whether our parents knew about our plans (2)**. I replied that it had even been our parents' idea. That surprised her, but she went on and **wanted to know how much time we had for our trip (3)**. I told her that we had all summer. I think she was quite impressed but then she asked all the questions we haven't talked about yet. She **asked when we wanted to leave (4)**, then **she wondered how much money we wanted to spend (5)**. When I told her that we didn't know, she sighed but went on and **asked whether we would go by train or by bus (6)** and **whether we wanted to visit National Parks or cities (7)**. Again I had to tell her that we didn't know. Then she became a little unfriendly and told me to go home and talk to you about these questions, and not to come back before we had answers and knew what we wanted.

5 14

Die *reporting verbs* sind auch hier frei austauschbar.

Erica: OK, let's start:

1. Christopher asked me **to find out what a Greyhound ticket from here to New York costs / will cost**.
2. He also **wanted me to check if we could / can / will be able to get off as often as we want to**.
3. Then **he asked me to find out more about Mesa Verde**.
4. He also **told me to see what there was on Chicago**.
5. Finally **he wanted me to hurry** up because he wanted to check his e-mail. Idiot!

Anna also had some interesting ideas. Let's see:

1. First she wanted me **to check where we could go by train.**
2. Then she **asked me to find out more about Kansas**.

Why is she interested in Kansas? It's so boring there. Anyway:

3. She also **told me to check on chat-rooms to find out more about travelling in the US**. That was a good idea.
4. Finally, she **wanted me to write an e-mail to the lady at the travel agency and tell her that she'd been / she had been very unfriendly, and that we wouldn't come back.**

Alright, that's it then.

6 15

Erica:

Alright, here's what I found out: A guy called Jason wrote that **we** should definitely travel through Kansas. He said that **he** had lived **there** all **his** life and **he** thought it was great! Unfortunately he didn't tell us what was great. Well, then there was a girl called Anne. She warned us not to go to Chicago. She said that **she** hated it **there** and that **she** had moved **there the year before**. She explained that all **we** would see **there** would be cars.
Then there was Allison. She was in Mesa Verde, and wrote that it was the greatest place of all. **They** had arrived **there the day before** and **she** hoped that **they** would stay until **the following Tuesday**. That was when there would be a special guided tour of the Native American sites. That sounds good. And finally there was a note by a guy called Joey. He said that **his** sister had come back from her trip **three days earlier** and that she had been very excited about the Great Lakes. **He** thinks she was crazy because **he** had been there **the winter before** and it had been freezing cold.
So what do you think?

7 16

Möglicherweise hast du andere *reporting verbs* gewählt. Das ist möglich und auch richtig solange du bedenkst, dass einige *reporting verbs* ein Objekt benötigen *(to tell sb, to ask sb)*.

1. *Anna:* Yes, – he told us **that he had lost everything** and **asked us to give him some money**.
2. *Christopher:* Oh, yes. That was the girl in Death Valley. She **said that her parents had forgotten her** and **wondered if she could come with us**.
3. *Anna:* She **explained that she would stay and live there** and **promised us that we would understand why three years later**.
4. *Erica:* Yes, **he said that he would give us (the girls) a ride** but he also **explained that he didn't take guys**.
5. *Anna:* Yes, that was interesting. That was the priest in Colorado. He **asked us whether we had thought about our lives** and **mentioned that someone might ask us soon**.
6. *Christopher:* Yes, how stupid. They **explained we would find everlasting love** if **we kissed there**.

Test

1

1. Yesterday my father **asked** me where the pictures of his trip through America were.
2. I answered that I **had** not **seen** them.
3. Then he told me not to be stupid and added that he was sure he had had them the day **before**.
4. I told **him** that I really wasn't interested in his pictures.
5. Then Dad said that he always kept them in **his** cupboard, but they weren't there.
6. Luckily, my mother came and **asked** why he didn't take the ones right in front of him and **leave** me alone.
7. My dad **said** that that might be a good idea and thanked my mother.

2

1. A man in 1875 said that travelling by train was dangerous because trains were too fast.
2. Last year a friend of mine told me that he/she was afraid of travelling by plane, and that her/his cousin had died in a plane crash five years earlier.
3. One of my classmates said that his/her mother had gone to America by ship the year before and she had loved it.
4. My pen friend from Australia told me that he would fly to the moon as soon as possible because he/she hated life here/there. (Both are correct in this case – *here* = on Earth / *there* = in Australia)
5. My brother asked me whether I knew how bad it was for the environment that everybody was flying around the world all the time.

American and British English 7

1 Check-up

	AE	BE
Would you like to see my apartment?	S	
Would you like to see my flat?		P
That's my favorite color.	E	
That's my favourite colour.		L
Can I use your bathroom, please?	L	
Can I use your toilet please?		I
Would you like to go to the theatre with me tonight?		N
Would you like to go to the theater with me tonight?	G	

An important difference between American English and British English is **spelling**.

2

My favorite place in the world

I once saw a **program** on television that showed a little island somewhere far away. I loved it. It was about 200 **meters** long and 100 **meters** wide. The water around it was incredible, too. The **colors** just made me go crazy. Green, turquoise, blue … In the **center** of the island stood a coconut tree about as tall as a house. They taste so much better than the ones you buy in the supermarket. In fact their **flavor** is totally different I think I would like to spend a holiday there without **neighbors** …

3 20 – 23

Sentence no.	1	2	3	4	5	6	7	8
BE	☐	☐	☒	☐	☐	☒	☒	☐
AE	☒	☒	☐	☒	☒	☐	☐	☒

Hörtexte

20

1. Could you pass me the butter, please? **(AE)**
2. Yeah, no problem. What are you going to do after breakfast? **(AE)**

21

3. No thank you, no coffee for me. I drink water for breakfast. **(BE)**
4. Really? I prefer tea – just like the English, [laughs]. Are you going to the waterside tonight? My friends and I want to have a swim. **(AE)**

22

5. You know, I think it's impossible to swim in that lake. The water is much too cold and I really don't understand how anyone could be stupid enough to jump in there. **(AE)**
6. Don't you, huh. I really don't understand why anyone couldn't. It's really refreshing. Apart from that, cold water is very healthy. **(BE)**

23

7. It's so hot today. I don't think I will be able to leave the house. I really have problems breathing in such temperatures. **(BE)**
8. Oh, come on. There are so many nice people here today. It's really not a good idea to stay home. Have you seen the hot girls from Las Vegas? I'm sure they would be disappointed if you didn't come along. **(BE)**

4

	BE	AE
filt	lift	elevator
sydiloha	holidays	vacation
mifl	film	movie
lupip	pupil	student
tetoil	toilet	bathroom
gorunundder	underground	subway
kram	mark	grade
mostpan	postman	mailman
psoh	shop	store
recerakat	caretaker	janitor

e	**m**	a	t	**g**	**r**	**a**	**d**	**e**	p	k
r	**o**	v	**v**	**a**	**c**	**a**	**t**	**i**	**o**	**n**
h	**v**	g	h	a	h	u	k	m	n	v
s	**i**	u	**s**	**m**	**a**	**i**	**l**	**m**	**a**	**n**
u	**e**	j	**t**	s	o	u	z	g	l	f
b	d	g	**o**	n	n	h	o	l	i	s
w	u	k	**r**	u	e	b	h	u	f	a
a	**e**	**l**	**e**	**v**	**a**	**t**	**o**	**r**	t	t
y	l	o	**b**	**a**	**t**	**h**	**r**	**o**	**o**	**m**
e	**j**	**a**	**n**	**i**	**t**	**o**	**r**	d	h	k
l	d	c	o	p	d	k	i	z	f	d
s	**t**	**u**	**d**	**e**	**n**	**t**	s	h	u	t

5

Hello Mum and Dad,

Yesterday I was in the city centre with some **pupils** from my class. We were **at the cinema**. It was great, although we had to **stand in a queue** for a long time for the tickets. The **film** was amazing (it was a horror **film**). It was about a **postman** who was attacked by a dog in the **back garden** of a house. The dog had jumped from a window on the **ground floor** onto the **veranda** and then almost killed the **postman**. After he had left hospital, he decided to kill the dog and went to the **shopping centre** to buy a gun. I don't think you'll want to hear the rest of the story, because it gets really scary. At school nothing really important happened, only that I lost my **exercise book**. So now I will get a bad **mark** for that class. I asked the **caretaker** if he had found it, but he hadn't. The **headmaster** of my cousin Sarah's **primary school** has decided that their summer **holiday** will be a week longer. I'm jealous. If I had a week more of summer **holidays** I would go to Las Vegas and win a lot of money for you.

Bye
Marc

Test

1 24

	AE	BE
1. Excuse me, where's the restroom, please?	x	
2. Just ask the caretaker. I'm sure he knows.		x
3. Does your brother go to primary school or to grammar school?		x
4. The car park is next to the shopping centre.		x
5. I'm in grade 10 at Lincoln High School.	x	
6. Let's take the subway downtown.	x	

2

Dear Mom and Dad,

Last week a **pupil** from my school gave a party. He lives **in the city centre** right next to the **theatre**. As a present I bought him the latest CD by his **favourite** hip-hop band. I had bought it at the **shopping centre** near school. The party was great. We were allowed to use the **veranda** and the **back garden**, and they let us dance until early in the morning. The **neighbours** didn't care at all, which was also great. In the **centre** of the lawn they had a little bar with soft drinks so we could take one any time we wanted. It was just great. Sometimes it's really nice to be in a house and not a small **flat** like we have back home in Manchester. Our **holidays** start next week and then my time here will almost be over. I have enjoyed it a lot. Thank you very much for giving me the chance to live here for a while. I have learned so many new things. I'm only afraid of my first English test back home. I'm sure I will get a bad **mark** because of all my American English. Well, life is not always fair, is it?

Love
Marc

Building words

1 Check-up

a)

to invite	invitement	**invitation**	inviting
to discuss	discuss	discussment	**discussion**
to move	movation	**movement**	moving
to surprise	**surprise**	surprising	surprisation

b)

certain	**uncertain**	incertain	discertain
possible	**impossible**	unpossible	inpossible
active	disactive	imactive	**inactive**
to lock	to dislock	to inlock	**to unlock**

2

to invite		**invitation**
-ing	-ation	
to butter		**butter**
-ment	—	
to combine		**combination**
-ation	-or	
to run		**runner**
-or	-er	
to nail		**nail**
—	-ing	
to travel		**traveller (BE) / traveler (AE)**
-ment	-er	
to end		**ending**
—	-ing	

3

employed		
im-	un-	**unemployed**

lucky		
un-	ir-	**unlucky**

correct		
in-	im-	**incorrect**

perfect		
un-	im-	**imperfect**

natural		
ir-	un-	**unnatural**

interesting		
un-	im-	**uninteresting**

exact		
un-	in-	**inexact**

active		
ir-	in-	**inactive**

4

joy	joyful *(positive)* / joyless *(negative)*
sense	senseless
wonder	wonderful
head	headless
life	lifeless
truth	truthful

5

Is cow tipping an exciting hobby?

1. To my **surprise** his **suggestion** was that we should go cow tipping.
2. He said that cow tipping was a **combination** of fun and exercise.
3. I then asked him for an **explanation** of what cow tipping exactly was.
4. Full of **excitement** he told me that the idea of cow tipping was to run against cows while they were sleeping, so that they fell over.
5. To his great **surprise** and **disappointment,** I said that this was not a good **treatment** of animals and that I thought that they needed **protection** from the kind of people who do such stupid things.

6

Cow tipping is a myth

I am a cattle farmer, and I have to tell you that cow tipping is **impossible**. It is a popular myth that city people invented to make fun of people who live in the country. It is **incorrect** that cows sleep standing up. They lie down to sleep. But even if they were standing, you would be **unable** to sneak up on them, because they would hear and smell you from far away. It is also highly **improbable** that you would be able to tip a cow – they are very heavy. As a matter of fact it would be extremely funny to see one of these town people running against a cow, bouncing off, and then being kicked in the head. I'm not sure if I would carry his **unconscious** body from the field. All in all I think it is **irresponsible** of people to invent stupid stories like this, but it is even more **unbelievable** that people believe them.

7

Opinions on cow tipping

1. I think cow tipping is great. It's an **inexpensive** way to spend your free time and it's a lot of fun. *(Joey, 18; Illinois)*
2. Cow tipping is a crime and it is **unforgivable**. *(Bill, 35; New York)*
3. What's the big **excitement** about cow tipping? Just accept that it's a joke that somebody made up. It's just a big **laugh**. *(Alice, New Jersey; 16)*
4. I think cow tipping is the most **irresponsible** thing anyone can do. I can't describe the **hate** I feel for the terrible people who perform **actions** like this. *(an animal rights supporter from Nevada)*
5. The people in my hometown in Oklahoma share the **belief** that cows are noble animals, and we should be more **respectful** towards them. Because of that we call all cow tippers "**killers** of the cows' honor". We believe that the **punishment** cannot be severe enough. *(Carl, 25; President of the "Honor the Cows' Honor Society", Iowa)*

Test

1

to mean	~~meanment~~	meaning
to number	number	~~numbertion~~
to swim	~~swimmor~~	swimmer
to use	useless	~~usefull~~
expensive	~~expenseful~~	inexpensive
possible	impossible	~~inpossible~~
end	~~endles~~	ending

2

How stupid can people be?

Have you ever heard about cow tipping? You haven't. Let me tell you: you're lucky. I'm one of the **unlucky** people who have. I spent my vacations in the **beautiful** state of Oklahoma, with its **endless** prairies and all these nice people. But then one day someone asked me what I thought of cow tipping. After he had explained it to me, I was **speechless** at first. Then I told him that this was the sickest thing I had ever heard of. We ended up having a long **discussion** about this totally **senseless** way of spending one's free time. He told me I couldn't talk about it if I hadn't tried doing it at least once. He was obviously **unable** to understand how someone could care for something as "**useless**" as a cow. All my **explanations** about animal rights and the correct **treatment** of other living beings didn't seem to affect him at all. Finally I just left the room and decided never to talk to this **impossible** person again. So if you ask me about the worst thing that happened to me during my vacation: this was it.

Claire

Reading comprehension 9

1 Check-up

A: b; **B**: a

2

Pike Place Market

Statement	true	false	not mentioned
a. Pike Place Market is a supermarket.		x	
b. Pike Place Market is expensive.			x
c. Pike Place Market is a good place for tourists.	x		
d. Pike Place Market is a good place for people from Seattle.	x		
e. Pike Place Market is a good place for teenagers.	x		

3

Seattle Center

Statement	true	false	not mentioned
a. Seattle Center is a zoo.		x	
b. Seattle Center offers many different kinds of activities.	x		
c. The most important building at Seattle Center is the Opera House.		x	
d. You can find a big wheel and a roller coaster at Seattle Center.			x
e. You can see very far from the top of the Space Needle.	x		

4

Here are examples of how you can guess the meanings of words – by looking at the parts of the words themselves, and also by looking at the words in context.

Word	Meaning	How did you guess?
fishmonger	Fischhändler/Fischverkäufer	*fish* + Zusammenhang
street performers	Straßenkünstler	Zusammengesetzt
delicacies	Delikatessen/Feinkost	Deutsch – Delikatessen
magician	Magier/Zauberer	Deutsch – Magier
spectacular	sensationell	Deutsch – spektakulär
to revolve	sich drehen	Zusammenhang
to zip up	hier: hinaufkatapultieren	Zusammenhang
waterfront	Hafenviertel / Stadtviertel am Ufer	*water* + *front*

5

Sandra: Excuse me, could you please help us with a few words?

Receptionist: Of course, young lady. Let's have a look at them.

Sandra: What are **area growers**?

Receptionist: Oh, these are farmers who have their farms near Seattle.

Philip: Thank you. And what about **artisans**?

Receptionist: They're people who make things with their hands – paintings, clothes, decorative or useful or beautiful things.

Sandra: Oh, of course. Now what's a **playhouse**?

Receptionist: That's a place where you go to see plays being performed.

Philip: Thank you very much. One last question: what's a **monorail**?

Receptionist: Well, it's something like a train, but it runs on only one rail, not on two rails.

Sandra: Thank you for your help. Good bye.

Receptionist: Anytime you have a question, please feel free to ask me.

6

Sandra: Hi, I'm Sandra from Germany, and this is my brother Philip. Could we ask you a question, please?

Marc: Sure, go ahead.

Philip: We've read these two flyers about Pike Place Market and Seattle Center, and we're not sure where we want to go. Which do you prefer?

Nancy: There's no question about it. Seattle Center is the best place. I loved the view from the **Space Needle** and the ride on the **elevator** – just 43 seconds – that's great.

Sandra: But isn't Pike Place Market fun, too – especially downstairs with all the **small shops**?

Marc: Yes, I agree. I like to do magic tricks and there's a great shop for **magicians' supplies**.

Philip: I think so, too. I really like reading. I could buy **comics and books**. And I also want to see these crazy people who throw **fish** until someone buys them.

Nancy: Oh, forget about reading and flying fish. Seattle Center is so exciting. All the great **rides** at Fun Forest. I just loved them.

Sandra: Hmm, now what are we going to do?

Marc: It's easy. Just go to both places. They're both near **the waterfront**.

Philip: Yeah, that's a great idea. Do you think Richard and Mary will like that idea?

Sandra: Well, I'm not too sure about that. They probably want to take us to some art museum.

7

German	False friend	False friend	German
Gewürzgurke	pickle	zit (AE) spot (BE)	Pickel
American Football	football (AE)	soccer (AE) football (BE)	Fussball
Bank (Geldinstitut)	bank	bench	Sitzbank
Hocker	stool	chair	Stuhl
Turnhalle	gymnasium	high school	höhere Schule
geschickt	handy	cell phone (AE) mobile phone (BE)	Handy
Küchenchef	chef	boss	Chef
schnell	fast	almost	fast
Bedeutung	meaning	opinion	Meinung
während	while	because	weil

b. I'm going to the bank.
c. I'm almost done/finished with my homework.
d. I would like to talk to your boss.
e. Could you please repair my chair?
f. Could you please pass me the pickles?

10 Listening comprehension

1 Check-up 25 – 26

1. 25

- [ ] On a plane approaching Chicago.
- [ ] On a plane approaching New York.
- [x] On a cruise ship approaching New York.
- [ ] On a tour of Chicago's harbour.

2. 26

- [ ] On a bus.
- [ ] In a private car.
- [x] In a taxi.
- [ ] On a motorcycle.

2 27 – 29

27

1. The radio show is about …
   - [ ] … theatre plays.
   - [ ] … movie stars.
   - [x] … musicals.

28

2. The commercial is about …
   - [ ] … tooth paste.
   - [x] … a lotion that helps against pimples right away.
   - [ ] … a lotion that cleans your skin.

3. The boy in the commercial is in a panic because …
   - [x] … his girlfriend will break up with him if he has got a pimple on his face.
   - [x] … his friends will not like him any more if he has got a pimple on his face.
   - [ ] … his mother will not let him go see a musical if he has got a pimple on his face.

29

4. How does the radio station show its listeners that musicals are interesting?
   - [ ] They interview an actor from a musical.
   - [ ] They interview teenagers whose parents have been to musicals.
   - [x] They interview teenagers who have seen musicals.
   - [x] They tell listeners about some musicals.
   - [ ] They give away free tickets.
   - [x] They play music from a musical.

3 30 – 32

H		B
B	M	H
H	B	H
M		M
M		H

4 33

- [ ] Where can I buy Broadway tickets?
- [ ] Can I order Broadway tickets before I get to New York?
- [ ] What colour are the tickets?
- [x] How expensive are the tickets?
- [x] How can I get cheap tickets?
- [ ] Is there a black market for tickets?
- [x] Why are some tickets cheaper than others?
- [x] Is it difficult to get tickets?
- [ ] Do I need a credit card to buy them?

5 34

	true	false	not mentioned
The enchanted prince looks like a beast until he finds a woman who takes him away.	x		
The prince's servants have also been enchanted to look like cups and other useful things.	x		
Belle had been looking for her horse when she found the castle.		x	
Belle likes the Beast from the beginning.		x	
The servants like Belle.			x
Gaston likes Belle.	x		
The people of the village don't want to help Gaston to attack the castle.		x	
Belle's father is afraid that Belle will be hurt.			x
In the end the Beast dies in Belle's arms.		x	

6 31

correct answer: No. 3

7 32

(6.) Eponine dies while helping Marius.

(4.) Jean Valjean decides to care for Cossette whose mother has died in a hospital.

(3.) Jean Valjean becomes rich.

(2.) Jean Valjean commits a crime again but is not caught and changes his name.

(7.) All the dead appear on stage singing.

(1.) Jean Valjean leaves prison after 19 years.

(5.) Cossette grows up and falls in love.

8 33

How to get Broadway tickets

- … fast:
  - expensive (up to $ 450)
- … not so fast:
  - cheap (starting at $ 20)
    1. ① Anyone Rush Tickets lottery Tickets for $ 25
    2. ② Partial View Tickets – most theatres sell them
    3. ③ Standing Room Only Tickets for $ 20
    4. ④ Wednesday Matinee Tickets between $ 5 and $ 20 cheaper than tickets for evening performances

disadvantages:

- ① It's a lottery, so you may not get a seat at all.
- ③ Like it says – you might have to stand for the whole show!
- ④ The tickets may still be expensive and you have to go in the afternoon.
- ② These aren't the best seats, so you don't see or hear everything.

Hörtexte

1 Check-up

25

1.

Captain: Good morning, ladies and gentlemen. Our wonderful cruise across the Atlantic is almost over now. We are approaching one of the world's greatest cities, also known as "The City That Never Sleeps". On your right you will soon see the Statue of Liberty, the symbol of this great country. We hope you enjoyed the cruise and we are looking forward to welcoming you on board our beautiful vessel again sometime. Please make sure you pick up your free tickets to a Broadway musical before leaving the ship. Thank you for choosing Trans Atlantic Cruises. Good bye.

26

2.

Ya know. I hate this city. Too many cars. It stinks. You wanna do my job here in this lousy place, you gotta be freakin' crazy. But I ain't got nothin' else to do. – Come on you idiot, the light ain't gettin' no greener – my wife always says: "Let's get outta here, let's go someplace quiet and peaceful. Then I laugh and say: "Who's gonna need a cab somewhere where it's peaceful and quiet? We're there, buddy – Broadway – you gonna see one of them stupid musicals? Man, you crazy. That's five bucks. Thanks.

2

27

This is New York's hottest teenage channel: TNY 96.5.

Hi, this is Sally O'Donnell, and today we're going to talk about something different – not about discos, not about movies, and not about the regular stars. No, today we're talking about musicals. No, don't turn off the radio! This is going to be exciting. Musical doesn't mean opera. Musical means great music, action and a lot of dancing, it can even mean horror – just wait and see. So, stay tuned and we'll find out some more after this message.

28

Boy: Oh my God, I've got a pimple on the tip of my nose. Jenny will dump me and all my friends will hate me!

Mother: Oh no, what can we do?

Boy: I'll kill myself! Look, it's all red and I look terrible. Oh, no!

Mother: Here, try to put some make-up on it. That'll cover it up.

Boy: No, mom – I'm not a girl! What if Jenny finds out I'm using make-up? Then it will definitely be over!

Fairy: A boy cries, with tears in his eyes? A mother screams – I know what that means. A pimple right in the face – oh, what a disgrace. Use anti-pimple super lotion and life will get back in motion.

Boy: Oh thank you, sweet fairy. Let's try it, mom!

Mother: Oh, look – it's gone!

Jenny (very much in love): Oh, hi Timmy, you look great! Let's go and see a musical. Oh, I love your skin so much …

Fairy: Anti-pimple super lotion – and life will get back in motion.

29

Sally: Alright then, I hope you've got your faces all under control so you can go see a musical. Many of you might think that musicals are boring, but we asked a bunch of teenagers leaving the theaters what they thought. Let's tune in:

Girl (crying): Oh my goodness, it was so sad, I can't believe she died – so beautiful *(sobs).*

Boy: Great music, I can't believe it. When my parents gave me the tickets for my birthday I thought they were crazy, but now I know what I want for Christmas – tickets for another musical.

Girl: It's amazing, just amazing. The stage with all the props and colours and the sound … It just blew me away.

Boy: The main actress was so beautiful and she had such a beautiful voice. I'm in love, I can't believe it!

Sally: That doesn't sound like a boring evening to *me*. But of course not all musicals are interesting for teenagers – some are more for adults. We're going to have a look at three of them – right after the next song, which is of course taken from a musical.

3

30

Sally: "Beauty and the Beast" is one of the most successful musicals on Broadway. It's named after the fairy tale – most of you probably know the story. For those of you who don't remember it, here's Andrew Jones to sum it up for you:

Andrew: Imagine you're a prince, cursed to look like a hideous beast – unless you can find a woman who really loves you. That's the situation the Beast finds himself in in this gripping love story. But it's not just the prince who's enchanted. His servants and everybody who lived at the castle at the time were turned into furniture, tea-cups, brooms or other objects needed in a castle. They are the first – well – *people* the beautiful woman Belle meets when she arrives at the castle. She's looking for her father, who's disappeared in the forest. Of course this leads to some very funny and entertaining moments, but the story also turns dramatic. Belle is at first afraid of the Beast, she's disgusted by such a hideous monster. But slowly she gets to know him, and she even starts to like him. At the same time the villainous Gaston, who wants to marry Belle, is looking for her. He finally finds her when she is out alone in the forest – once again looking for her father. When Gaston finds out that she doesn't want to marry him, and that she's been to a castle inhabited by a beast, he and the people of the village attack the Beast's castle. Gaston fights with the Beast and wounds him with a knife, but he dies himself. As the Beast lies there, wounded and dying, Belle tells him that she loves him, and kisses him. The spell is broken – the wound is healed – the prince and Belle are in love. The rest is a party. "Beauty and the Beast" is an evening full of enchantment, fun, great costumes and music and, last but not least, dramatic tension and a great story. Don't miss it!

31

Sally: Thank you, Andrew. I think I'll check that one out as soon as I get tickets. A very different love story is presented in "Little Shop of Horrors," a musical that has been on stage since 1982 and is still popular. Mary Lockwood watched it last night. And I can tell you – she was scared!

Mary: A flesh-eating plant, a guy who cuts people to pieces with a chainsaw, and a dentist who loves nothing more than seeing his patients in pain? This sounds more like a horror movie than a musical, doesn't it? Well, "Little Shop of Horrors" is the story of Seymour, a poor orphan who works in a flower shop in a poor area of New York. He's in love with Audrey, a poor and naïve girl who's involved with the sadistic dentist, Mr. Mushnik. One day, during a total eclipse of the sun, a strange plant appears that will change Seymour's life forever. From the day

Seymour brings the plant into his shop, business, which had been very bad, suddenly booms. Being a smart young man Seymour soon discovers that it was the plant that changed everything. He also finds out that all the plant needs to survive is … *human blood*. First he feeds it with blood from his fingers, but as the plant grows it gets bigger – and hungrier. It wants more blood, and sings the song, "Feed me, Seymour". Seymour becomes famous because of the plant, and also finds out how badly Mr. Mushnik is treating Audrey. He accidentally kills Mr. Mushnik in a fight and decides to feed him to the plant, which he calls Audrey II. Audrey, now rid of Mr. Mushnik, becomes Seymour's girlfriend. The plant keeps on growing, though, and finally Seymour realizes that it has come to Earth to eat all humans and take over the world. He fights the plant … but loses. In the end both he and Audrey are eaten by the plant. Finally a musical without a happy ending! But this musical has amazing, very modern music, lots of action, and a plot that will make you look twice at every plant you pass.

32

Sally: I wonder how Mary slept last night. Now from horror to history – "Les Misérables" is another musical that's been successfully performed on Broadway for more than ten years. This one will really make you cry! Alice Hansen was there and can tell you more about it.

Alice: If you've never cried in the theatre, go and see "Les Misérables". Be it because of a poor mother selling her hair and turning to prostitution to save her daughter's life – be it because of good people dying on the barricades, fighting for their rights – or be it because of the heroine's father's death, after having done everything to escape his terrible past – "Les Misérables" is a must-see musical! It's set in 19th-century France, where Jean Valjean has spent 19 years in prison for having stolen bread to feed his starving family. After leaving prison he commits another minor crime, but escapes capture and begins a new life under a new name. He becomes rich and decides to care for the child of a dying woman. The girl, Cossette, grows up and falls in love with a young man called Marius. Marius is a revolutionary fighting for the rights of the people. Yet he is also loved by another woman, called Eponine, who is tragically shot while helping Marius deliver a message to Cossette. In the end everybody dies while fighting for their rights, except for Cossette and Marius. In the final scene the dead return to the stage, singing the revolutionary song they were singing before the fighting began: "Do you hear the people sing, singing the song of angry men, it is the music of a people who will not be slaves again …" And yet, they have died for nothing.

4

33

Sally: (crying) … Oh my goodness, that was so sad. I've actually seen this one myself, and it was unbelievable … well, now that we've told you so much about the musicals, we should tell you about the ticket situation, too. Peter went to Broadway to find out more.

Peter: Hello everybody. The good news is: it's really easy to get tickets for a musical here on Broadway. The bad news is, you have to have a lot of money if you want them fast. You can actually pay up to $450 for a single ticket. However, if you invest a little time and don't need to sit in the best seats, you may get to see the same show for just $20. Of course it'll cost you time instead of money if you want to get the tickets cheap. Here are a few ways to get them: first there are the so-called Anyone Rush Tickets. This is a lottery for a small number of tickets, held a few hours before the show starts, so you have to be there on time and take part in the lottery. If you're lucky, you'll get a ticket for around $25. If you're unlucky – well, you'll have to watch a movie instead. Another way is to buy tickets for seats from which you might not see part of the stage. These are called Partial View Tickets. Most theatres sell tickets in that category. So if you're willing to miss part of the action, or if you don't mind the sound not being so good, this is the way to go. There are also Standing Room Only Tickets. For around $20 you'll get into the theatre – but you might not get to see the show sitting down. You can take a seat if you can find one that's empty, otherwise you'll watch the musical standing up. Keep in mind that most musicals last around three hours. Finally, it might be a good idea to watch a Wednesday matinee. Most musicals are shown on Wednesday afternoons (usually starting between 2 and 3 p.m.). These are usually between $5 and $20 cheaper than tickets for the evening performances. This may still be expensive, and you'll have to go to the theatre in the middle of the day. Of course, the cheapest way to get tickets is asking your parents to pay for them, but it might be easier for them to buy your tickets if you gave them a few good cheap tips.

Sally: Thank you Peter. Now you know everything there is to know about one of the greatest forms of entertainment to be found in New York. My name is Sally O'Donnell from TNY 96.5 – the hottest teenage station on the air. I'll be back tomorrow with the first reports from our listeners who are going out tonight to see a musical. So be sure to tune in.

Inhalt der Audio-CD

Track	Page	Unit, Exercise	Title
1	20	Unit 1, Ex 6	Talk on the trail
2	36	Unit 2, Ex 10	They discuss their plans
3	57	Unit 4, Ex 2	Visitors from Germany
4	58	Unit 4, Ex 3	What to do in Chicago
5	59	Unit 4, Ex 4	The Schusters have arrived
6	61	Unit 4, Ex 6	After their tour of Chicago
7	62	Unit 4, Test, 1	Time to say good bye
8	62	Unit 4, Test, 2	Time to say good bye
9	63	Unit 6, Test, 3	Can Jennifer and Ken go to Germany?
11	76	Unit 5, Test, 3	Alice is afraid of the next class test
12	83	Unit 6, Ex 2	Planning a trip to America
13	86	Unit 6, Ex 4	At the travel agency
14	88	Unit 6, Ex 5	Checking the internet
15	90	Unit 6, Ex 6	A homepage on travelling in the US
16	92	Unit 6, Ex 7	Holiday photographs
17–19	101	Unit 7, Wissen	Unterschiede in der Aussprache BE und AE
20–23	104	Unit 7, Ex 3	Unterschiede in der Aussprache BE und AE erkennen
24	107	Unit 7, Test, 1	Unterschiede in der Aussprache BE und AE erkennen
25	130	Unit 10, Ex 1	What are the people saying? Where are they?
26	130	Unit 10, Ex 1	What are the people saying? Where are they?
27	132	Unit 10, Ex 2	Radio show: Anmoderation
28	132	Unit 10, Ex 2	Werbung
29	132	Unit 10, Ex 2	Interviews
30	133	Unit 10, Ex 3	Summary "Beauty and the Beast"
31	133	Unit 10, Ex 2	Summary "Little Shop of Horrors"
32	133	Unit 10, Ex 2	Summary "Les Misérables"
33	133	Unit 10, Ex 4	Report: How to get Broadway tickets

Register